On the Thirteenth Stroke

Surrealist Poetry in Brita

Michel Remy was born in Epinal, France, and educated at the University of Nancy. He has taught in French universities since 1970, specialising in modern art and literature, and is currently a professor at the University of Nice. He founded the surrealist review *Flagrant Délit* (1980–85) and participated in the activities of the Phases movement in France and the Melmoth Group in London. The author of *Surrealism in Britain* (Ashgate, 1999), Remy has published and lectured extensively on British surrealism. He has co-curated several exhibitions and is the author of many articles and prefaces to exhibition catalogues in France, Britain and elsewhere. He is an occasional consultant to Christie's on matters relating to British surrealism.

Surrealist writing available from Carcanet Press

John Ashbery, *Collected Poems 1956–1987*
John Gallas, *The Book with Twelve Tales*
Barbara Guest, *Selected Poems*
Federico Garcia Lorca, *Four Puppet Plays*
Pierre Martory, *The Landscapist: Selected Poems*
Edwin Morgan, *Collected Poems*
Octavio Paz, *Collected Poems 1957–1987*
Raymond Queneau, *Elementary Morality* and *Hitting the Streets*
James Tate, *Selected Poems*
The Humphrey Jennings Film Reader, edited by Kevin Jackson

On the Thirteenth Stroke of Midnight

Surrealist Poetry in Britain

Edited by Michel Remy

To Susie, my quicksilver wife

To Nicolas and Lisa, my phosphorescent children

First published in Great Britain in 2013 by
Carcanet Press Limited
Alliance House
Cross Street
Manchester M2 7AQ

Selection, introduction and editorial matter copyright © Michel Remy 2013
Acknowledgements of permission to reprint individual works, given throughout the
book, constitute an extension of the copyright page.

ISBN 978 1 84777 109 4

The publisher acknowledges financial assistance from Arts Council England

Typeset by R. J. Footring Ltd, Derby
Printed and bound in England by SRP Ltd, Exeter

Contents

Contents

Contents

Contents

Acknowledgements

This anthology would never have been possible without the help of a large number of friends, booksellers, archivists, collectors and artists, all surrealists or enthusiasts for surrealism, all remarkably disinterested, who for many years have blazed the sunken trails of surrealist poetry and shown the way to the mines and reefs of gold and silver.

Among them, I want to thank more particularly the copyright holders of the poets whose texts, often given to me purely out of friendship and fellow-feeling, I have gathered and treasured over the years.

My warmest gratitude also goes to Michael Schmidt and Carcanet Press, who have not hesitated to throw their energy and expertise into this adventure, and especially Judith Willson and Helen Tookey who have sailed the boat to its berth.

To Desmond Morris and John Welson, among the staunchest heirs to surrealism in Britain, all my thanks. They have both been indefatigably supportive of the project since its inception and Desmond Morris has generously contributed to its illustrations.

The assistance of these many collaborators has enabled the generosity and resilience of the surrealist spirit to be expressed once more in its undeniable permanence.

List of Illustrations

Introduction
Hearts on Fire in the Snow
A Brief History of Surrealism in Britain

The 'entrance of the mediums' into Britain – that is, the gradual introduction of surrealist ideas and principles into the British art and poetry of the thirties – has been described so often and so extensively in prefaces to exhibition catalogues and articles in various journals that it will suffice here to recall its main stages, especially as no precise date can be assigned to the starting point of the movement in Britain. Indeed, the year 1936, which was the official foundation date of the 'Surrealist Group in England' and marked the launch of its activities, can be rightly considered as the year that demonstrated definitively that surrealism had *already* permeated Britain. A few months after the close of the mammoth International Surrealist Exhibition at the New Burlington Galleries in London in June 1936, André Breton wrote that 'this exhibition marked the highest point in the graph of the *influence* of our movement', and noted that London had become the centre of 'the objectivisation and internationalisation of surrealist ideas', which were reaching 'their critical point here'. He added:

> Taking into consideration the specifically English sources from which, for centuries, sensibility has sought refreshment, I was persuaded that surrealism had drawn from them deeply enough to have nothing to fear. Sooner or later it will be discovered that it has sought to carry with it all that is most fertile in the art and literature of the past, so that it was obliged to pay a considerable tribute to the literature and art of England.[1]

A few critics see Vorticism as the forerunner of surrealism in Britain, and it is true that the breakthrough made by Vorticists such as Wyndham Lewis was their attack on the dogmas of representation and the political dimension of their aesthetic protests; but they retained a literal approach to reality, celebrating its dynamic forces and its tangibility. One has to wait for Unit One in June 1933 – an ephemeral group which brought together abstract artists such as Barbara Hepworth, proto-surrealists such as J.S. Bigge and John Armstrong, and pre-surrealists such as Paul Nash and Henry Moore – to see the criticism levelled at conservatism in art reach its peak. That same year,

---

1 André Breton, 'Limites non frontières du surréalisme', *Nouvelle Revue Française*, February 1937. Translated by Franklin Rosemont and included in *What is Surrealism? André Breton, Selected Writings* (New York: Monad, 1978).

the courageous Mayor Gallery exhibited Francis Picabia, Paul Klee, Jean Arp, Joan Miró and Max Ernst in April and held a one-man show by Max Ernst in June, attracting scathing criticism from the whole of the press – just as Anton Zwemmer's exhibition of Salvador Dalí's drawings and oils had in 1934. It is also true that the London Film Society had paved the way with its exclusive screenings of René Clair's *Entr'Acte*, Germaine Dulac's *The Seashell and the Clergyman*, and Man Ray's *Emak Bakia*, *The Starfish* and *The Mystery of the Château de Dé* from 1926 to 1930, supported by *Close-Up* and *Film Art*, two avant-garde film reviews. Lending support to all these ventures were three key magazines. Eugene Jolas' *transition* and Edward W. Titus' *This Quarter* were both Paris-based but both had a circulation of about 1000 in Britain and both published English translations of French surrealist poems. (The 1932 issue of *This Quarter* was entirely devoted to French surrealist texts and illustrations, placed as it was under Breton's editorship). Meanwhile in London Geoffrey Grigson's *New Verse* published the first English surrealist poems by David Gascoyne from 1933 onwards.

The 1936 exhibition

When Eileen Agar, Roland Penrose, Julian Trevelyan, David Gascoyne, John Banting and Humphrey Jennings, who had made frequent stays in Paris and had befriended most of the French surrealists while visiting Stanley W. Hayter's Atelier 17, all found themselves back in London in 1935, it seemed that the situation was ripe. That year, David Gascoyne published *A Short Survey of Surrealism* and translated André Breton's *What is Surrealism?* The decision made by David Gascoyne and Roland Penrose 'to do something in London', when they met by chance in Paris for the first time in July 1935, through their mutual friendship with Paul Eluard, materialised with the setting up of the organising committee of the International Surrealist Exhibition, under Herbert Read's presidency, with the collaboration of André Breton in Paris, Salvador Dalí in Spain, E.L.T. Mesens in Brussels and Vilhelm Bjerke-Petersen in Denmark.

The exhibition ran from 11 June to 4 July, recording a total of 25,000 visitors, and certainly was surrealist in its subverting of the usual rules of cultural decency and social habits. Sheila Legge walked through the streets down to Trafalgar Square with a mask of roses covering her face, a pork chop in one hand and an artificial leg in the other – a perfect surrealist phantom, as the press reported with relish. Lectures were given to a bemused public, with André Breton clad entirely in green, Herbert Read standing on a sofa and interrupted by a bell every five minutes, and Salvador Dalí famously imprisoned in a deep-sea diving suit in the stifling June heat, until David Gascoyne managed to unscrew the helmet. Dalí continued to lecture from slides shown upside down and in utter disorder, while Dylan Thomas went round with boiled string in a cup, asking people, 'Do you want it weak or strong?' Meanwhile the fourth *International Surrealist Bulletin* was issued, and the Surrealist Group in England was formally launched. Among the first initiatives was the resounding 'Declaration on Spain', a vibrant protest against the British government's policy of non-intervention in Spain, published as a broadsheet in the November 1936 issue of *Contemporary Poetry and Prose*.

Politics and aesthetics

Apart from Roger Roughton's *Contemporary Poetry and Prose*, which mainly published avant-garde, mostly surrealist, poetical texts, there was no official organ of the Surrealist Group before the *London Bulletin* was launched in 1938. The group's political position filtered through in several articles by Herbert Read in *Left Review*, in which surrealism sided with, but refused to adhere rigidly to, the doctrines of the Communist Party. Its political stance was visible in its collaboration with the annual exhibitions organised by the Marxist-inspired Artists' International Association. In this sense, the group followed the response Breton gave to the Tenerife review *Indice* in 1935. Asked whether art could put itself into the service of a definite political idea, Breton answered that

> it must unreservedly put itself in the service of that idea during the period in which the idea is transformed into action but ... it is indispensable that art should regain its independence if the artist wishes to escape serious contradictions objectively harmful even to the idea which he wishes to serve.[2]

In 1937, on the occasion of a huge exhibition organised by the AIA for 'the Unity of the Artists for Peace, Democracy and Cultural Development', the group issued the manifesto 'We Ask Your Attention', a strongly argued indictment of the government's policies printed on a broadsheet and illustrated by Henry Moore. The following year, under E.L.T. Mesens' leadership, the group published Breton and Trotsky's 'Towards an Independent Revolutionary Art' in the December 1938–January 1939 issue of the *London Bulletin*.

It was indeed the moment of taking sides, and all exhibitions organised by the group had a definite political dimension. Mesens and Penrose financed the exhibition of Picasso's *Guernica* and its 67 preparatory drawings at the Whitechapel Gallery in October 1938, an exhibition opened by a jobless working-man picked at random from the street. The proceeds of the exhibition were sent to Spain in aid of the women and children of the Republic, as with Max Ernst's show in December the same year, whose proceeds were

---

2 Interview given in May 1935 on the occasion of an International Surrealist Exhibition in Tenerife; published in André Breton, *Position politique du Surréalisme* (Paris: Editions du Sagittaire, 1935).

sent to the aid of the Czech and Jewish refugees from Central Europe. In January 1939, the *Living Art in England* exhibition at the London Gallery, which gathered surrealists and constructivists, raised funds for the same cause. But the actual political standpoint of the group is better defined by its organisation of the *Surrealism Today* exhibition at the Zwemmer Gallery in June 1940. The show opened on the very day in which the Nazis entered Brussels, a coincidence interpreted by the *Observer* newspaper to reveal the surrealists' 'ignorance of what heroism and the nobleness of the human soul may mean'. Surrealism was not prepared to compromise with the forces of obscurantism.

The war

The war was a difficult period for the group. In the spring of 1940, Mesens tried to reinforce the ideological integrity of the group by asking its members to commit themselves exclusively to surrealism – a pledge which Ithell Colquhoun, who was engaged in occult research, and Grace Pailthorpe and Reuben Mednikoff, whose psychoanalytical work was leading them into other circles, refused to make. In the same year, the group's members were dispersed on account of wartime duties. Besides being ARP wardens, Penrose, F.E. McWilliam and Julian Trevelyan were engaged in camouflage work, with McWilliam subsequently joining the RAF. Conroy Maddox worked in a factory in the Midlands, and J.B. Brunius worked at the BBC. In 1942, Toni del Renzio, who had arrived from France at the outbreak of the war, tried to bring everyone together with his publication of *Arson*, which included the paintings of Emmy Bridgwater and John Melville as well as his own. But Del Renzio's intimacy with Ithell Colquhoun and his editorship of a surrealist section in *New Road 1943* irritated Mesens, who saw in him a would-be Breton and a plagiarist. A violent dispute, conducted through letters and articles in *Tribune* and *Horizon*, ensued between Mesens, Penrose and Watson Taylor on the one hand and Del Renzio on the other. In 1944 this gave rise to two pamphlets of a singular virulence, *Idolatry and Confusion* (Mesens) and Del Renzio's reply, *Incendiary Innocence* (both reproduced in this volume).

From the end of that year, collective activity began to re-emerge from the ashes of the war, with *Message from Nowhere*, *Fulcrum* and the *Surrealist Diversity* exhibition at the Arcade Gallery in 1945, coinciding with the discovery by Penrose and Mesens of the outsider artist 'Scottie' Wilson. This regrouping culminated in 1946 with the publication by Simon Watson Taylor of *Free Unions Libres*, which brought together texts and illustrations by French and English surrealists. A year later, the final appearance of the group as such was on the occasion of the International Surrealist Exhibition at the Galerie Maeght in Paris: a declaration was drafted and signed by fourteen English surrealists, a blend of anarchists, first- and second-generation surrealists and fellow-travellers of the group. The declaration stated, once again, the group's commitment to the proletarian revolution and to the principles laid down by Breton twenty years or so before. In 1949, Mesens and Penrose organised an exhibition of Desmond Morris's works at the London Gallery. In 1951, the gallery closed down, a victim of the lack of cohesiveness of the group and the lack of interest on the part of the general public. Mesens and Penrose were engaged in the founding of the Institute of Contemporary Arts, but the former soon withdrew, unwilling to engage to such an extent with 'officialdom'.

The permanence of the surrealist spirit

Surrealism lay dormant for sixteen years. It reawakened in 1967 with the *Enchanted Domain* exhibition organised in Exeter by Mesens, Brunius, Maddox and a newcomer, John Lyle, a committed and enthusiastic bookseller. The show brought together 50 artists from several countries and from different periods of the movement, some ever-present since its inception, others – such as Anthony Earnshaw and Patrick Hughes – having recently joined. This led to the launching of John Lyle's review, *TRANSFORMAcTION*, which featured the work of Philip West, Glen Baxter, Tony Blundell and Ian Breakwell, among others.

Ten years later, in London, Conroy Maddox formed the Melmoth group with John Welson, Paul Hammond, John Digby, Tony Pusey, Roger Cardinal, Michael Richardson and Francis Wright, and published a short-lived magazine of the same name. The *Surrealism Unlimited* exhibition, organised by Maddox in conjunction with Edouard Jaguer's Phases movement at the Camden Arts Centre in January 1978 as an answer to the more official Dada and surrealism review exhibition at the Hayward Gallery, did not suffice to strengthen the links between the members of the group. Since then, perhaps the most serious attempt to maintain surrealist activity in England has centred on the Manticore group in Leeds, with Kenneth Cox, Sarah Metcalf and Bill Howe; while John W. Welson and Neil Coombs in Wales, Desmond Morris in Oxford and Kathy Fox in Kent continue, by way of a kind of occultation, to maintain the flame and permanence of the surrealist spirit.

Surrealism, considered by Breton to be 'the very prehensile tail of romanticism', is, I would argue, an essential part of the English literary canon. What is has contributed is not the fantasy found at the bottom of a treacle well or when bumping into a dong with a luminous nose, but a revelation of what is irreducible in *otherness*, an incompleteness that demands constant questioning and redefinition. Surrealism in Britain shares the essential intransigence, the anonymous, drifting quality of surrealism in general. In its spirit of revolutionary freedom, it has been a secret necessity – felt, if not always avowed – of British writing. To borrow the title of one of Roland Penrose's poems, included in this volume: surrealism in Britain has been, and continues to be, a road wider than long – at times contracting, at times expanding, but a road that will continue to follow its own inimitable course.

'For the Snark was a Boojum, You See'
An Assessment of Surrealist Poetry
in Britain

It has to be said, first and foremost, that any attempt to assess the 'quality' or 'value' of surrealist writing in comparison with other writing – such as that by T.S. Eliot, Dylan Thomas or James Joyce – is in total contradiction with the nature and goal of the surrealist proposition and with its most fundamental principles. By definition, surrealist writing eschews the traditional criteria (taste, beauty, structure, depth, symbolism…) by which one judges a piece of writing, for the good reason that the movement in itself does not propound a style or a set of writing techniques, but is rather a body of commitments, a state of mind, a unilateral declaration of independence. Surrealist writing is based on the dislocation of meaning for the sake of the emancipation of the mind and its unabashed, unfettered expression. Breaking with the usual ways of assessing a piece of writing, we may state that the 'quality' of a surrealist text, then, is proportionate to its resistance to univocity and to its inexhaustible power of creating *astonishment*.

It is true that, compared with painting, writing has not been the main activity of the surrealists in Britain; nonetheless, there is an abundance of texts, albeit often hard to come by. Some of these texts were published in little reviews, now almost impossible to track down; most of them have never been published and have been retrieved from personal archives: if the British group was, understandably, the only one in Europe able to pursue its activities during the Second World War, nonetheless the economic conditions and national preoccupations, as well as the dispersion of the members of the group, did not favour any kind of publication. However, as this anthology reveals, these texts show astonishing variety, iconoclastic force and remarkable visionary quality, almost as if the lack of editorial and commercial constraints had allowed the perfect mental freedom necessary to 'the dictation of the subconscious'. Uncompromising, spontaneous revolt against literary norms can be seen in the work of all the writers included here, who employ and exemplify a range of surrealist strategies in order to open 'the gates of horn and ivory', in Nerval's phrase.

The precipitation of images and the principle of non-contradiction: David Gascoyne, Toni del Renzio, Simon Watson Taylor

David Gascoyne's poem 'And the Seventh Dream is the Dream of Isis', published in the December 1933 issue of Geoffrey Grigson's *New Verse*, can be seen as the first ever surrealist poem published in English. Indeed, the reading process which it demands sets the tone for all surrealist writing in Britain: reading is a permanent hesitation, the site of a challenge thrown down by the signified to the signifier, a process of deferral and the refusal of any single referent. The poem precipitates images of destruction and desecration, unfolding images of the infinite clashing with the finite and suspending the very principle of contradiction. Isis' dream is the dream of the reader: to gather together all fragments in the hope of finding an unfindable unity. David Gascoyne's texts replace the teleological process of significance (aiming at a predefined end) with the incantatory process of desire. This process telescopes cause and effect and opens up the infinite possibilities of writing, based on endless displacement and decentring.

This displacement appears also in the litanies of Toni del Renzio and Simon Watson Taylor, their texts exemplifying a form which is the place of pure rupture. Indeed, it initiates a movement of words which plays so much on contradictions that it eventually exemplifies the principle of non-contradiction itself, recalling Breton's words: 'I believe in the future resolution of those two states, apparently contradictory, dream and reality, into a kind of absolute reality, a surreality, if one may say'. Del Renzio's texts set this movement of ever-postponed resolution at the service of love and the act of love as liberating the self from all kinds of authority, especially the paternal. Simon Watson Taylor's texts are grounded in the proliferation of double and triple genitives embedded into one other, words endlessly created from words, onto which improbable adjectives are grafted. The writing gathers pace through the unstoppable lengthening of the lines, creating remote echoes which crush the perspective. Writing is shown to be a drama which bounces off itself, in constant celebration of its birth and its demise, testifying, *a posteriori*, to an incalculable subversive force. These texts are flamboyant funeral orations, hymning the ephemeral almightiness of the word.

In fact, this notion of mourning, which might remind one of André Breton's own statements concerning the 'continuous misfortune of automatic writing', is central to all British surrealist texts – paradoxically associated with the notion of origin, or, better, origination. Most British surrealists write in this inbetweenness, in an intermediate verbal space inspired by the concepts of life in death and death in life so central to romanticism, epitomised for instance by Coleridge's mysterious poem *Kubla Khan*. Surrealism is, as Breton declared, 'the prehensile tail of romanticism, a most prehensile tail'. It is perhaps significant that the texts most illustrative of this double force of mourning and origination are those written by the female members of the group.

The revolt against univocity: Len Lye, Conroy Maddox, Desmond Morris, John W. Welson, Hugh Sykes Davies, Anthony Earnshaw, George Melly

The revolt against univocity and against the institutions which encourage and maintain univocity pervades the texts of poet-painters such as Conroy Maddox, Len Lye, Desmond Morris and John W. Welson. Emblematic of Conroy Maddox's writing is his 'The Playgrounds of Salpetriere' (also the title of a later painting by Maddox), referring to the hospital in Paris where Professor Charcot and his assistants studied the behaviour of 'hysterical' women at the end of the nineteenth century. In this text, hysteria is located at the heart of the writing process, as the spasmodic expressions of the body and the unconscious in their joint challenging of the power of logic. More intense in their organic quality, Desmond Morris's texts animate the inanimate, anthropomorphise objects and deconstruct the self, astonished by its latent – and tranquil! – violence. One is aware in each text of the presence of Morris the entomologist and ethologist, the dissector of the body of reality – as also shown in his drawings and oils – for whom all things are connected in reciprocal relations and turn back on themselves in a permanent process of mutation. Deep down, almost as a complement to Desmond Morris's dissecting visions, John Welson feels the irrepressible force of desire as the driving principle of such dissection and mutation, the desire for the other which fragments us. His are splintered texts, full of teeth, eyes, lips and knives. Brief lines, short stanzas and aphoristic form convey the impression that we are torn away from the illusory wholeness of mental and social life alike – a strategy also used to similar effect by George Melly in his few rare poems.

Aphorisms can be among the most pungent forms of indictment, and Anthony Earnshaw is a master of aphorism, precipitating realities against each other and turning our rationalities upside down. Earnshaw makes us accept the unacceptable, brilliantly demonstrating that humour can be a powerful strategy to subvert conformist ideas.

Emblematic of these strategies of subversion, and of the unsettling of rational certainties, Hugh Sykes Davies' poems, and the extracts included here from his novel *Petron*, confront us with the blank which lies at the core of any writing but especially surrealist writing – the inaccessibility of any ultimate meaning and hence the groping of the mind for some elusive logic on which one could ground oneself and feel secure.

In the same way, logic is submitted to an iconoclastic treatment in Len Lye's dislocated texts, in which we seem to witness the sudden and chaotic emergence of thought from the blanks between words. The spaces in these texts are full of circulations, echoes, paronomasia and sinuosities pointing towards an inaccessible origin, hence the near-untranslatability of the texts. As in Joan Miró's paintings, the reader is made a witness of the inception of meaning and the origin of consciousness.

The fading prospects of origins: Emmy Bridgwater, Edith Rimmington, Ithell Colquhoun, Reuben Mednikoff, Grace W. Pailthorpe

Emmy Bridgwater, Edith Rimmington and Ithell Colquhoun walk the tight-rope between eros and thanatos. In Bridgwater's case, her obsession with birds corresponds to the circularity characteristic not only of the flight of birds – which soar up into the sky but must always return to the earth – but also of the opening and closure of the act of writing. Bridgwater's texts teem with ellipses, anacolutha, hypallages and interjections – so many fragments of lost analogies. They also display sudden changes in linguistic register, from the lyrical to the familial, from the trivial to the oracular. All the lexical and syntactic hiatuses send us back to the original blank in which all births take place. Similarly, Edith Rimmington's brief, sometimes aphoristic texts, most of them automatic, create discontinuous chains of meanings, echoes and paradigms, the result of physical and mental breathing, her texts ebbing and flowing always at those margins where elemental and animal forces disrupt the subject's authority, leaving him or her both an entity and a non-entity, as if permanently mesmerised by otherness. Ithell Colquhoun also gives us an indication as to what governs the fracture of, and in, reality, creating a slow, repetitive, carefully descriptive and irresistible work which makes us pass on to the other side. In her texts, the point of departure is always located in a solid, concrete, orderly world – an everyday life scene circumstantially described. Details comfort us, give us confidence in the solid reality she describes; but gradually, almost imperceptibly, an 'unsaid' is revealed, the text turning back on itself like a 'chev'ril glove' whose 'wrong side may be turned outward ... quickly'. This is seen for instance in the image of the house she wants to rent in the heart of London, one room of which opens on to 'the crash and smother of Atlantic waves, breaking ceaselessly and without tide'. At the core of Colquhoun's writing lies a fascination with the passage to the other side of the mirror, a descent into the world of myth and arcana, especially Celtic. Her *Goose of Hermogenes* (1961) depicts an initiatory journey in which she gives an alchemist's vision of the transmutation of things. Here, writing is Becoming.

Correspondingly, the jointly written poems of Grace Pailthorpe and Reuben Mednikoff are transcriptions of the phantasmatic fears, obsessions and rejoicings of their authors. What is crucial for Mednikoff is the *breathing* which the poem retraces, in the hope of facing those fears, an echo of the poet's anguish when confronted with the fantasy of castration. The automatic resurgence of erudite and long-forgotten words, or the invention of apparently Latinate words, is an attempt to reach back to the origin of language and thought and, through this delving, to come to terms with the subconscious. The self is in quest of reconciliation with itself, through a kind of re-linking of itself with the past, of the body to the body of the other, of blood with milk at the moment of a new, eagerly expected birth. Pailthorpe's poems, in the same way, celebrate the moment when pain views its own liberation, a wished-for explosion or delivery, the latter a paradoxically apt word for a childless artist whose paintings display a fascination with infants and foetuses.

Calls to revolt and the liberation of desire: Roland Penrose, Roger Roughton, Jacques B. Brunius and E.L.T. Mesens

The word is the key necessary to open the world's secrets. In the texts of David Gascoyne and Simon Watson Taylor, each line starts the process of dislocation of meaning. In Roland Penrose's poems, each line also throws back to the reader bits and pieces of a reality grasped at the moment of its foundering. Penrose asks us to accept the loss of reality so that desire might be liberated. In his texts, space opens on to the infinite, landscapes have human – especially feminine – shapes and writing is eroticised, a locus of desire and hope. This is most apparent in his extraordinary poem *The Road is Wider than Long* (1939), a montage of poetical texts printed in various fonts, fused with photographs taken by Lee Miller and himself. The work is a topographic and amorous itinerary in quest of his own love for Miller, a chronicle of the blurring of all kinds of limits. In Penrose's texts, images of corruption, rottenness and rupture vie with images of transformation, passage and reversal: a double-faced image, a dialectic without synthesis, a 'fire of sorrow and hope'.

More overtly militant, Roger Roughton's texts illustrate his attempt to create a dialectical synthesis between the hopes of those who are oppressed and the promises of the surrealist revolt. Roughton's texts are full of latent revolt and irony – especially in the parodic, even mocking, use of rhymes, and in the alternation of the material and tangible on the one hand, and poetical visions on the other – or the everyday on the one hand and the transhistorical on the other. Roughton's texts are calls to turn away from all academic traditions, calls to the future, calls to a revolt on both the discursive and the imaginative plane.

Similarly, the poetry of Belgian-born E.L.T. Mesens, the 'leader' of the English surrealist group and director of the London Gallery, can be seen as a poetry in action, one that tears away the claims of any moral order, stigmatises what is banal and mediocre, demystifies deep-rooted beliefs in conformist values and attacks all forms of conservatism, taking a bitter stand against social and political forces, resisting the absurdity and inequality of a complacent world based on money, religion and human stupidity. Mesens' poetry is the epitome of the militant libertarianism at the heart of surrealism, British or otherwise. The same could be said of French poet and filmmaker Jacques B. Brunius, whose poems here included were written while he was in England, having fled occupied France, working for the Free French forces radio on the BBC. His iconoclasm cannot be separated from a radical belief in the power of the individual to love freedom and life.

The quest for collective memory: Humphrey Jennings

The process at work in Humphrey Jennings' writing sees the ephemerality of human activities at the core of the permanence of natural forces, and vice versa. His poems are moments in time, experiences of the instant, monuments in which the past records its own meanderings. Mostly entitled 'reports', Jennings' texts both pretend to adopt the objectivity of an observer and start a slow movement of descent towards hidden layers of meaning, as if they were taking advantage of the fractures and interstices of reality. The reader slips from one category to another, reaching down to a kind of collective memory, beyond history into myth, revealing the creative energy of humankind, confronted not so much with the invisible as with the not-yet-visible. Jennings' great achievement was his *Pandaemonium*, a gathering of texts by poets, essayists, novelists and philosophers, celebrating the machine throughout the ages and testifying to the deep organic impulse which links the machine, the human being and his or her subconscious.

This is exactly what this anthology aims to reveal: the radical belief in the freedom of the individual and in the human being's capacity to change the life of his or her mind. I have chosen not to classify the texts according to thematic categories or sources of inspiration, such as 'nature' or 'love', as some traditional anthologies do. The reason is simple: it is more in keeping with the spirit of surrealism not to stress what could – however tenuously – link this writing to the themes and forms of more conventional poetry but to emphasise what separates it from them. However forgotten, neglected or underestimated it might have been, surrealist poetry in Britain, like surrealist poetry in France, Czechoslovakia or Belgium, participates in the inexhaustible revolt against the diktats of discursive logic and in the general strategy of dislocation by which the reader is led to suspend all pre-established codes, including those of his or her own mental habits. Surrealist poetry knows no national borders: it is international in outlook; and this, paradoxically, is one of the things most clearly revealed by this anthology of surrealist poetry in Britain. In exploring the writings collected in this book readers will, I hope, experience for themselves the writers' desire to hear at last the thirteenth stroke of midnight.

A Note on the Texts

Some of the poems included here were first published in small-press magazines or books, often now difficult to locate. The majority are published here for the first time. I have therefore included as much information as possible, for each poet, about the provenance, dates of composition and previous publication status of the texts. Those texts here published for the first time have been sourced from the authors' private papers and estate archives. It is in the same spirit of authenticity that I have reproduced most of the manifestos as they were originally printed.

As with any anthology, the choice of the texts results from the editor's own criteria. In this case, the guiding principle has been to give full respect to two surrealist exigencies: first, the genuine and attested involvement of the author with the English surrealist group and its activities; and secondly the capacity of the individual poem to demonstrate the subversive power of the language of surrealism.

Manifestos and Declarations of Surrealism in Britain

First English Manifesto of Surrealism
A Fragment

This text was written by David Gascoyne in French in 1935. It was published in Christian Zervos' art magazine *Cahiers d'Art*, which was extremely sympathetic to surrealism. Gascoyne was at the time engaged in writing *A Short Survey of Surrealism* and in translating André Breton's *What is Surrealism?* It is a paradox typical of surrealism in Britain that this text has never previously been translated into English. It is subtitled 'A Fragment', which might suggest that Gascoyne wrote a more complete version, but there is no evidence of such a version ever having existed.

Surrealist groups exist everywhere in Europe, in America, in the Canary Islands and in Japan. Only England remains – although one of the last non-Fascist countries – a country where such a group is missing. The time has come we should fill up that void.

Let us first proclaim our determination to sacrifice nothing to what is generally speaking called 'the great English tradition'. In vain will our adversaries wield that scarecrow in the discussion. Surrealism is not an exotic addition which this tradition would accept or reject. It is not a literary school, it is an international system of ideas determined by the particular conditions of our time. Let it be said, however, that we recognise our precursors in Swift, Edward Young, Monk Lewis, William Blake and Lewis Carroll and that we also salute all the writers alive who have devoted themselves to the cause of the revolution. But we want to affirm our independence from all the foreign 'standards' of criticism. Our intention is to resolutely follow our own path, regardless of the attacks which are levelled at us from so many individualist literati as well as from the International Writers' Association.

At the moment we are writing this (May 1935) in London, the whole of England, led by the capitalist press, prepares for the Jubilee, one of the most nugatory and sickening explosions of hysteria. Isn't it a symptom of historical justice: when a country is invited by its government to such a parody of rejoicings in the name of patriotism and imperialism, despair is the poets' first reaction.

SURREALISM IS THE DIALECTICAL SOLUTION TO THE PROBLEM OF THE POET.

While giving great importance to the class struggle, surrealism is, by essence, opposed to the 'leftist' attitudes, according to which 'proletarian' literature and propaganda art are the only revolutionary art. The poets who deserve that name would have only one choice: either the pursuit of a simplified, popular, 'proletarian' art whose aim would be its propagandist efficiency, or a non-political, highly subjective art, whose aim would be the mere individual expression of its author. But surrealism indicates a third way, the only valid one, which triumphantly leads away from the traps of the first two. We, surrealists, believe in a future when the Revolution will reveal the real, the surreal range of all the faculties of life, love and thought, when all its shackles will be for ever broken. Poetry cannot fuse with propaganda. It is an act through which man reaches the most complete knowledge of himself.

THE GOALS AND METHODS OF SURREALISM

Surrealism's fundamental ambition is to abolish the formal distinction between dream and reality, between objectivity and subjectivity, so that, from the distinction of all those old 'antinomies', there emerges in full daylight the future state of things for which all revolutionaries fight.

The means used by surrealism to reach this goal are, first and foremost, automatic writing and the experiments on the nature of automatism. Surrealism is an instrument through which a universal, pure voice is heard. Surrealist texts only express thoughts being born, thoughts unarrested by reason and logic. Important theories on surrealist techniques have been developed over the past ten years.

'To compare two objects as distant as possible from each other or, through any other method, put them in the presence of each other in a sudden and startling way, remains the highest task of poetry. Its unique, unequalled power must be exerted to reveal the concrete unity of the two terms thus associated and to communicate to each of them a force which it lacked all the while it was considered singly. What must be broken down is the downright formal opposition of the two terms. What has to be overcome is the apparent disproportion between them, which only fosters the infantile, imperfect idea one has of nature and the externality of time and space. The stronger the idea of immediate dissimilarity appears, the quicker it must be overcome and negated. The dignity of the object is here at stake. Thus, two different bodies, rubbed together, give a spark and reach supreme unity in the fire, and steel and water reach a common, admirable resolution in blood, etc. An extreme intrinsic particularity cannot be an obstacle to this way of seeing and feeling:

in the same way, architectural decoration and butter are perfectly combined in Tibetan *torma*, etc.' (André Breton)

THE DECLARATIONS OF SURREALISM

1 – We declare ourselves in total agreement with the principles of surrealism as they were first stated by André Breton. 2 – Relying only on the proletarian Revolution to achieve the liberation of Man, we here solemnly adhere to the historical materialism of Marx, Engels and Lenin. 3 – We are of the opinion that England offers to surrealism a vast field of poetical, artistic, philosophical, … action. 4 – We commit ourselves indefatigably to the fight against fascism and war, imperialism, nationalism, humanism, liberalism, idealism, anarchistic individualism, the art for art's sake theory, religious fideism and, generally speaking, any doctrine coming from a party or an individual which capitalism could make use of to try and justify its continuation.

David Gascoyne

Declaration on Spain

The Spanish Civil War broke out in July 1936. Surrealists worldwide, and many left-wing groups and parties, immediately expressed their support for the Republicans. This broadsheet was published in 1936 together with the sixth issue of *Contemporary Poetry and Prose*, inserted as a central page in the magazine. The signatories constitute the core of the first surrealist group in England. At the moment of its publication in November, Roland Penrose, his wife Valentine Penrose, and David Gascoyne were in Spain, accompanying Christian Zervos, the editor of *Cahiers d'Art*, on a mission to establish whether art works discovered in churches, cathedrals and the houses of exiled or executed fascists were being protected. In Barcelona, Gascoyne worked for Radio Catalonia, translating news bulletins and broadcasting them to the rest of Europe.

DECLARATION on SPAIN

Against the appalling mental and physical suffering that the Spanish Civil War is involving, we can already offset certain gains to humanity which will remain whether the Government of the People conquers or not; gains of knowledge which have been purchased far too dearly, but which for that very reason have an imperative claim on our attention. They are these:

1. No one can continue to believe that, if a People's Government is elected constitutionally, Capitalism will be content to oppose it only by constitutional means.

2. No one can continue to believe that violence is the special weapon of the proletariat, while Capitalism is invariably peaceful in its methods.

3. No one can continue to believe that Fascism is a merely national phenomenon. It is now abundantly clear that in a crisis the Fascist countries emerge as parts of an international whole, the International of Capital. German and Italian arms are killing the people of Spain.

4. No one can continue to believe that Fascism cares for or respects what is best in humanity. In Garcia Lorca, the foremost modern poet of Spain, they have assassinated a human life which was especially valuable. Meanwhile the People's Government have made Picasso director of the Prado, hoping to widen still further the scope of his work for humanity.

5. No one can continue to believe that our National Government has any right to speak in the name of democracy. It has assisted in the crime of non-intervention; it has refused to allow the export of arms to a Government democratically constituted, and has regarded with equanimity the assistance given by Fascist powers to the rebels. There can be no more conclusive proof of its real sympathies than its conduct towards Portugal. Portugal is a British financial colony, and depends on British arms for the protection of its overseas possessions. A word from our Foreign Office would have secured her immediate adherence to the pact of non-intervention. Evidently that word has not been given. The National Government has permitted the Portuguese dictatorship to assist the rebels in complete freedom; at every stage of the campaign the rebel armies have been based on the Portuguese frontier.

If these things are clear, we are the gainers in so far as we know *inescapably* where we stand with regard to Fascism, to the People's Government, and to the National Government of Britain. And in the light of this knowledge we support the popular demand that the ban on the export of arms to the Spanish Government be lifted. We accuse our National Government of duplicity and anti-democratic intrigue, and call upon it to make at once the only possible reparation

A R M S
for the People of Spain

Hugh Sykes Davies, David Gascoyne.
Humphrey Jennings, Diana Brinton Lee,
Rupert Lee, Henry Moore, Paul Nash,
Roland Penrose, Valentine Penrose, Herbert
Read, Roger Roughton.

Issued by the Surrealist Group in England.

We Ask Your Attention

This broadsheet was published and widely distributed on the occasion of the First British Artists' Congress, organised by Nan Youngman, Quentin Bell and Viscount Hastings in April and May 1937. Parallel to the Congress, a huge exhibition was mounted by the Artists' International Association. Rooms were devoted to the various artistic tendencies and styles, one of them to 118 surrealist works, of which 43 were by British artists. The broadsheet, printed on both sides of a yellow paper, featured a text overprinted with a majestic design by Henry Moore. The surrealists reveal here their political maturity and seriousness of purpose.

On the occasion of the Artists' International Congress and Exhibition

WE ASK YOUR ATTENTION

NON-INTERVENTION is not merely a political expedient in the Spanish situation, nor the alleged policy of a certain international committee. It is something much more than that ; it is the typical and inevitable product of a way of thinking and behaving, the prevailing political attitude of **educated and conscious** people since the war.

This attitude has been pure NON-INTERVENTION. Politics were looked upon as a dirty and stupid game of little real importance. Politicians were paid off to play it on their own, recognised knaves and professional liars, but not too sharply questioned as long as things went not too outrageously, and above all as long as the intellectuals were left safely with their books, their arts and intellectual interests. Their aim was **to localise politics**, to confine it to a few people, to treat is as a possibly contagious, certainly disgusting disease.

This attitude has been modified in one direction only. Memories of the last war, and the obviously growing dangers of another, have produced widespread pacifism. For the pacifist tries to deal with war as an isolated disaster, apart from its wider causes and connections ; he tries to look upon it as the embodiment of an abstract principle of VIOLENCE, and he will try to oppose it by the equally abstract principle of REASON. He will not examine the actual social and economic circumstances which produce violence, and above all he will not seek to oppose it by actual political means ; he will not meet it on its own ground. He remains NON-INTERVENTIONIST.

In a similar way the London Non-Intervention Committee was designed to apply this policy in the situation created by the international Fascist coup in Spain. Political expedience and political justice were ignored ; all social and political circumstances were disregarded, in favour of a single object : to localise the conflict, to confine within limits as narrow as possible this outbreak of VIOLENCE.

In this way the London Committee has a significance far beyond its own immediate aims. It is a practical test, a crucial experiment upon the attitudes which we have adopted. Is it possible to remain blind any longer to the results of this experiment ?

The facts, the events, are not in dispute. The Fascist countries, Italy, Germany and Portugal, have assisted Franco freely with materials of war and barely disguised divisions of their regular armies. They have condescended to cloak their actions to some extent under promises, agreements, denials and counter-charges. But behind this fog of words, Fascist intervention has proceeded unhampered save by the magnificent courage of the armies of THE SPANISH PEOPLE.

Is there any reason to suppose that Non-Intervention at future times and in other places may succeed better? Has Fascist militarism announced any limit to its hopes of conquest? Has it shown signs of a moral regeneration, of a greater respect for agreements and conventions? The opinion of the politicians at least is clear. Since the Fascist outbreak in Spain every European country

has hastened and enlarged its plans of re-armament. Only a few pacifists continue to believe in Non-Intervention. By doing so, they can only assist the forces of war by yielding one strategic point after another to the militarist dictators, they make VIOLENCE more certain and intimately more disastrous in its effects.

One thing, then, is clear. With all respect for the motives of pacifism, for the sincerity and courage of pacifists, this form of Non-Intervention is completely discredited in practice by the Spanish experiment.

But more depends on the experiment than this. Not only pacifism has been on trial, but our whole attitude of Non-Intervention in politics. How have our paid knaves and liars conducted themselves?

Unfortunately, like paid knaves and liars. If, conceivably, six months ago NON-INTERVENTION was defensible, it was only remotely justifiable as long as there was a fair fight between the parties in Spain. The German and Italian invasions removed even these remote justifications. At the very least we might have expected unequivocal protests against the Fascist aggressors, but even these have been lacking.

Unfortunately, this is not all. Our Government has in various ways intervened actually on behalf of the Fascist aggressors. Several weeks before the international ban on volunteers, it dug up a century-old Act on Foreign Enlistment, and indicated its intention to harass British volunteers gratuitously by this antiquated instrument. It has repeatedly refused to admit representatives of THE SPANISH PEOPLE, and their friends, at the same time allowing free passage to Franco's financial agents. And clearest of all, it has negotiated its famous " gentleman's agreement" with Mussolini, an agreement which apparently includes a free hand for Fascism in Spain. Our present hired rulers, in fact, so far from being Non - Interventionists, stand as the **allies of fascism** in international politics.

This is the result, in international affairs, of our NON-INTERVENTION; we find ourselves allied, not with the countries of peace and democracy, but with the countries of war and dictatorship. Has our attitude produced a more satisfactory situation within our own country? The publication of the Re-armament programme must remove the last possible illusions. Having sabotaged all hopes of collective security in the League (remember Simon and the Japanese attack on Shanghai; the Hoare-Laval pact) we must now become a great military power. Having failed to evolve any constructive economic policy to deal with general UNEMPLOYMENT and the Special Areas, we must now pour a gigantic loan into the pocket of heavy industry and armaments, to maintain a sham face of prosperity.

Worse, if possible, than the programme itself was the way in which it was introduced. Only a year after the Peace Ballot elections "honest" Baldwin himself announced in the House of Commons that he had intended to re-arm all the time, and that he deliberately concealed this intention from the electorate because he feared that they would not approve of it. This is the end of democracy and representative government; it is a FASCISM which uses deceit instead of violence.

And that is the result of our NON-INTERVENTION at home. We find ourselves ruled by a Fascism of deceit now, but signs are not wanting that force will follow. By an iniquitous Trades Disputes Act the political strike has been made illegal. The Sedition Act has ensured the creation of a mercenary army accessible only to capitalist political influence. The recent Public Order Act has given the police practically complete power to suppress all undesired political activities.

At the same time steps are being taken to ensure militarisation and organisation of the civilian population. A campaign for physical fitness, a tightening of control on the essential means of propaganda, a fixation of warlike ideas and images by the farcical pageantry of the Coronation—FASCISM, though still only Fascism by deceit.

We have no longer any excuse. NON-INTERVENTION in all forms must end. Artists, intellectuals, all people who live consciously, must recognise their political responsibilities, above all, their duty of direct political action in defence of their own interests. Do not let us deceive ourselves further; in a militarised state the activities which we value, the kind of consciousness which produces them, cannot exist. " **A warlike state,**" said Blake, " **cannot create.**" Setting aside general questions of democracy, justice, humanity, we are forced to defend the bare opportunity to carry on our work.

Intervene—but how?

First, unity among ourselves. We are no longer advancing the views of individuals, or of groups. We are defending our common interests and necessities.

Second, activity within the appropriate organisations. We welcome particularly the Congress of British Artists, organised by the Artists' International Association. We hope that it will find time to take up a clear position towards broader political problems, and consider possibilities of political action. Other organisations to which we would draw attention are: Association of Writers for the Defence of Culture; " For Intellectual Liberty"; International Peace Campaign.

Third, we recognise that we are not alone; we are not even the first to realise that the whole political life of the country is at the beginning of a crucial period. Within the Labour Party, the Trades Unions, and the working classes generally there is a new vitality, a new consciousness of the dangers which threaten us all. In spite of the weakness (and worse than weakness) of the old Labour leadership, the movement for a United Front is gaining ground rapidly.

The means of intervention in the political field are well defined by the parties of the UNITED FRONT. We have everything to hope for in supporting a vigorous policy according to their plans and nothing to hope for from any other party. If only in self-**defence we must END ALL FORMS OF NON-INTERVENTION, INTERVENE IN THE FIELD OF POLITICS, INTERVENE IN THE FIELD OF IMAGINATION.**

THE REVOLUTION which we can bring about must have as its object the DEVELOPMENT OF CONSCIOUSNESS and the WIDER SATISFACTION OF DESIRE.

Economic justice is the first object of our intervention, but we demand also the vindication of the psychological rights of man, the liberation of intelligence and imagination.

INTERVENE AS POETS, ARTISTS AND INTELLECTUALS BY VIOLENT OR SUBTLE SUBVERSION AND BY STIMULATING DESIRE.

Eileen Agar
Hugh Sykes Davies
D. Norman Dawson
Merlyn Evans
David Gascoyne
Erno Goldfinger
G. Graham
Charles Howard
Joyce Hume
Rupert Lee
Henry Moore
Paul Nash
Roland Penrose
Herbert Read
Julian Trevellyan

Published by the Surrealist Group and printed by the Farleigh Press (T.U.), 17-29 Cayton Street, E.C.1.

'No Dream is Worse than the Reality in Which We Live'

This text was published in the last issue of the *London Bulletin* (18–20 June 1940) as a broadsheet. This call to go beyond the drab reality of the world emphasises the political involvement of the Surrealist Group in England and its indefatigable belief in the forces of renewal intrinsic in human beings.

NO *dream is worse than the reality in which we live.*

No reality is as good as our dreams.

The enemies of desire and hope have risen in violence. They have grown among us, murdering, oppressing and destroying. Now sick with their poison we are threatened with extinction.

FIGHT

HITLER

AND HIS IDEOLOGY
WHEREVER IT APPEARS

WE MUST

His defeat is the indispensable prelude to the total liberation of mankind.

Science and vision *will persist beyond the squalor of war and unveil a* new world.

To the Workers of England

This text, strikingly presented with an aggressive yet clear typography, was published and distributed along with the *London Bulletin* at the beginning of 1939. It listed its warnings and injunctions in black ink on orange paper.

TO THE WORKERS OF ENGLAND

THE GOVERNMENT IS ASKING

YOU

TO CARRY OUT ITS

RE-ARMAMENT PROGRAMME

FOR WHAT PURPOSE ?

ARE YOUR EFFORTS TO BE TO HELP FASCISM ?

POWER is in YOUR hands

UNITE and USE IT

MAKE YOUR CONDITIONS. INSIST ON A
DEMOCRATIC FOREIGN POLICY AND

ARMS FOR THE SPANISH PEOPLE

UNITE ! DICTATE YOUR TERMS

THE WORLD IS ALREADY AT

WAR

FIGHT

FOR	AGAINST
FREEDOM of speech, thought, and expression.	**REPRESSION** or encroachments on the rights of individuality
CO-OPERATION with Progressive Parties and DEMOCRACIES.	**FASCIST IDEOCRASIES AGRESSION** wherever it may occur.
DISARMAMENT moral, material and universal.	**MILITARISM** in all its forms.
INTERNATIONAL understanding and interests.	**NATIONALISM** economic wars, national jealousies.
RIGHTS OF MINORITIES and small nations.	**IMPERIALISM** military or commercial.
REVISION of antiquated systems; education, the churches, family life, marriage and divorce, charity.	**REACTION** The safeguarding of high finance, imperial and vested interests, hereditary privileges.
WIDER CONSCIOUSNESS	**BLIND ACCEPTANCE** of the present state of
REVOLUTION	**INJUSTICE AND MISERY.**

BEWARE!

The next "War to end War" will be fought for "Democracy" and the "Empire."

Remember what to Fight for.

Issued by The Surrealist Group in London

Idolatry & Confusion

This leaflet was published privately in 1944 by E.L.T. Mesens and Jacques B. Brunius with the agreement of Roland Penrose, as an attack on propagandist, engagé poetry and, beyond that, on what was seen as Toni del Renzio's pretension to act as the holder of the surrealist 'doxa', especially after his editorship of the surrealist section of poetry in *New Road 1943*.

The text published below was meant for publication in "TRIBUNE", in an attempt to dispel some of the confusion created by recent articles, reviews and letters printed in that weekly. It was refused. Having found nowhere else a free forum, we are obliged, as a makeshift, to publish this text ourselves.

Idolatry & Confusion

"Patriotism is the last refuge of a scoundrel."
                                             Dr. JOHNSON
                                  (*Boswell's Life of Johnson*) 1887.

"Toute l'eau de la mer ne suffirait pas à laver une tache de sang intellectuelle."
                                  LAUTREAMONT (*Poésies*).

Was it not a mistake that the article on "Literary Idolatry" by Arthur Koestler[1] was not written by a Frenchman? Whatever may be Koestler's knowledge of France none but a writer, French in expression and formation, could throw much light on this subject (which seems to have been wantonly obscured) provided that he was, as much as Koestler and even more, free from the current political and literary conventionalities.

It is not without circumspection that we have decided to intervene in a debate in which we greatly risk having to oppose all the opinions already expressed.

Koestler will understand, as he wrote at the end of his article: "Others who could legitimately speak in the name of France are silent. They know as the Chinese proverb says, that there is a time to go fishing and a time to dry the nets."

In spite of their apparent discrepancies, the various articles and readers' correspondence, inspired by the publication in England of certain French texts of a more or less temporary interest, have *something* in common: this is the ignorance, the confusion, and the obliteration by sentimentality of all sense of values.

Lack of sense of values is one of the basic elements of what Koestler aptly calls "French 'Flu". Since 1940 there have appeared but few texts in French of any importance. In the first rank among these are:

1. "Lettre aux Anglais" by Georges Bernanos (Atlantica Editora—Rio de Janeiro).
2. The Interview given by André Breton to "VIEW" on his arrival in the United States. (No. 7-8—October 1941).
3. "Prolégomènes à un troisième manifeste du Surréalisme ou non" by André Breton. (VVV No. 1.—1942—New York.)
4. "Situation du Surréalisme entre les deux guerres" by André Breton. (VVV—No. 2-3—1943—New York.)
5. "La Part du Diable" by Denis de Rougemont (Brentano's—New York.)

(*N.B.*—This short list places itself above all sectarianism.)

None of these books and articles made the least stir in England, not even "Lettre aux Anglais" which deserved, by its title, rather more attention. Why was this book not translated and published in Great Britain?

What, on the contrary, have we heard about from the foremost English critics? Of topical poems written by the ghost of Jean Aicard who signs Aragon; of *Silence de la Mer*, the sort of story which the French daily papers published before the war, *Silence de la Mer* about which there has been such a commotion only to conceal its distressing emptiness.

Lack of sense of values. Mrs. Naomi Mitchison, in her letter to "TRIBUNE", adds to the dossier of the discussion a pamphlet unknown to English readers entitled *L'Honneur des Poètes*. These four pages are highly interesting, paved with good intentions and with a great many very bad poems. It is a psychological document that "propaganda" has hastened to use, perhaps rightly. But there is a long step from war-propaganda to poetry. Those who, stupidly or per-

[1] TRIBUNE—November 26th 1943.

26

fidiously, persist in confusing the poet's honour (—patriotic?—religious?—humanitarian?—) with the eternal function of poetry are liable to receive full in the face these lines by Arthur Rimbaud whom they profess to admire :—

Tout à la guerre, à la vengeance, à la terreur.
Mon esprit! Tournons dans la morsure : Ah! passez,
Républiques de ce monde! des empereurs,
Des régiments, des colons, des peuples : Assez!

But Mrs. Mitchison satisfies herself with discovering in *L'Honneur des Poètes* what she calls "new rhymes" and with advising us to read Aragon "not as politics but as poetry". New rhymes? *Fers* rhyming with *refaire*? Is this really what the English poets are after? As for Aragon's "poetry", it is a clever music-hall lyrics technique, unquestionably at the service of a double-faced policy.

Arthur Koestler was perfectly right in saying that the English poet who dared to use the words "my fatherland", "my soul", "my heart", etc., would cover himself with ridicule in the eyes of the same intellectuals who go into ecstasies over *Le Crève-Cœur* or an unimportant story like *Silence de la Mer*. British propaganda has not had to pluck too hard at the string of patriotism at home. It would have been a mistake. Realistic slogans, on the other hand, have had a great success. "Food Facts", "Dig for Victory", "Hit Back", "Salvage", and so on, need no Rudyard Kipling. If Aragon were English he would probably be unable to command the smallest consideration as a propaganda-poet, and would be reduced to sharing with Lords Elton and Vansittart the tiny patriotic-poetic rectangles in the "SUNDAY TIMES."

* * *

Why all this agitation about doubtful goods and silence as to what really matters? No doubt it is largely because Bernanos, Breton and de Rougemont do not glorify the various conformisms fashionable in wartime, and because they arouse the spirit of criticism. There is something else : they have had the good fortune to escape from the European fortress. This is apparently a redhibitory defect for literary men. The curiosity of the intelligentsia is excited by the writer in a cage. How will the oppressed writer behave? The critics and the public peer at him with a mixture of well-justified pity and a rather tainted curiosity. If Aragon was on view at the Zoo what crowds we should see. Yet the lovers of queer animals have not deigned to cast a look at André Malraux, though he too is in the cage. "LETTRES FRANCAISES" (Buenos Aires) and "FONTAINE" (Algiers) have published texts by him which are by no means negligible. Why has nobody noticed them? Why has nobody broken out into hysterical contortions in his honour? Whether one is an admirer of Malraux or not, whether one agrees with him or not, objectively his texts are worth far more than "J'ai sept ans et j'apprends l'Histoire de France" versified by Aragon.

Confronted with so much incoherence, we can but welcome the first healthy reaction : Koestler's article published in "TRIBUNE". Though this article calls for all sorts of reservations which we will attempt to set forth here as clearly as possible, it has the merit of being the first to denounce the new snobbishness now in fashion, and the "blackmarket in literature." But whether it is denounced or not, you will see that this is not the end of the "blackmarket"; that there will be others which will make literary capital, political capital, and indeed just capital, of the French resistance. If only the Belgians had an Aragon, even a minute one, you would see what you would see! But apparently they have nothing but "poètes maudits", except for a few traitors, and the archpriests of officialdom.

* * *

The tragic confusion which reigns in the world to-day has not failed to affect literary and artistic circles in all countries. It does not do, therefore, to exaggerate the dangers of the "French 'Flu" from which some English critics are suffering. But what is irritating is that their erratic judgments are constantly added to by gross factual errors, by chronic historical inaccuracies and incessant demonstrations of ignorance, all aggravated by the journalists' mania for talking with assurance of things he knows nothing about. Without attempting to compile the thick volume which would constitute an anthology of these mistakes, one can make an edifying list of them in a few minutes.

Let us first take the case of Aragon : here you have Kathleen Raine eulogising Aragon—1940 in "THE LISTENER" (No. 745). She confuses his surrealist with his communist activities. She thinks that as a communist and a surrealist he was a writer of "moderate talent" and qualifies these two activities as "the niceties of surrealism or communism", adding that surrealism "was based on a largely heartless defeatism—a kind of intellectual *schadenfreude*".

In the article in "TRIBUNE" Koestler, too, undiscerningly mixes up Aragon's surrealism and communism in order to attack him the more easily, and he recovers some indulgence only when he adds to his oddly-assorted bouquet the present poetic and patriotic logorrhœa of the same personage.

The same confusions are the rule in both camps.

Nevertheless, anyone who wanted to know has had the opportunity of learning that Aragon ceased to be a surrealist, and repudiated the surrealist manner of thinking when he plunged into the "niceties" of Stalinism in about 1931. But it is not because Aragon-Stalinist started to write vulgar doggerel and perpetrated the stupid articles in "CE SOIR" dedicated to Fernandel, Jeanne d'Arc and Maurice Chevalier, considered as representatives of the French "genius", that one should forget that he previously wrote *Anicet, Le Libertinage, Le Paysan de Paris*, and *Traité du Style*, that this same Aragon had been one of the most brilliant minds of the post-war period. The fact that he has become prematurely senile detracts nothing from his past. It is for this reason that it is regrettable that Koestler should encourage, unconsciously or not, the usual historic mistakes or lies when he dates the use of technical and scientific terms in poetry from 1930, and that he should give the credit to W. H. Auden and his group . So much the worse for Koestler if he does not know Lautréamont; but we refuse to believe that he is ignorant of the poetry of Walt Whitman and Emile Verhaeren; so much the worse for him if he has not read Guillaume Apollinaire's *Alcools* and *Calligrammes*. As for Aragon, his first texts date from before 1920, at which time Mr. Auden and his friends were still lapping their small beer at their big schools. If people are going to reconstruct contemporary history with such ingenuity we must be prepared soon to learn that Augustus John preceded Henri-Matisse, that Lord Berners was the precursor of Erik Satie, that Benjamin Britten was Strawinsky's master, and that the sad and murky Graham Sutherland numbers among his pupils a callow young man named Picasso.

The first attack on Aragon was published in "NEW ROADS" 1943. Unfortunately it was a lamentable one. A gentleman called Toni del Renzio accused him of signing a manifesto with Déat, and this is most probably false. ·

Mr. Calder Marshall, on the other hand, defends Aragon as a patriot in "TRIBUNE" (No. 357, October 29th, 1943). It is quite possible that Aragon is a patriot, of the same kind as Marshal Pétain, for example. It is extremely curious to observe that not one of Aragon's English admirers has taken the trouble to read carefully and to the end one of the "poems" in *Crève-Cœur* entitled "Complainte pour l'orgue de la nouvelle barbarie". Here is a fragment:

> . . . Nous voulions partir mais non
> Sans larmes sans espoir sans armes
> Ceux qui vivent en paix là-bas
> Nous ont dépêché leurs gendarmes
> Ceux qui vivent en paix là-bas
> Nous ont renvoyés sous les bombes . . .

Translated into simple language this means, precisely: "These English swine have let us French down at Dunkirk. They prevented us from going on board with them in their flight. They live in peace in England, and they sent us back beneath the bombs, driven back by their military police." This is exactly one of the lines of propaganda most used by Pétain, Laval, Déat, and so on. But doubtless the English admirers of Aicaragon had already dozed off to the delicious purring of his "poetry".

Enough of the patriot. We note in passing that Mr. Calder Marshall takes Mr. del Renzio for a surrealist. Another mistake.

Let us go on to Eluard. Cyril Connolly, in his lecture given in Edinburgh, and subsequently printed in "HORIZON" (No. 42, June 1943), among pathetic appeals for a greater literary entente with France, and many pertinent remarks, spoke of the "patriotic poems" of Paul Eluard. We should be curious to know in which poem of *Poésie et Vérité* 1942 Connolly was able to discover the slightest trace of patriotism. He must have mixed him up with Mr. Aragon-Déroulède. As for Mr. Ranci del Conno's letter to "HORIZON" (No. 48, December 1943) he speaks of the "versification" of Eluard. He must have confused him with Mr. Aicard-Aragon. At the most there can be found in Eluard's work since 1920 a single poem using rhyme and metre. This poem is called "L'égalité des sexes" and dates from 1924. And what, in any case, does Mr. Conci el Rondeau know of the reasons the surrealists had for using rhyme or not. Attempting to make up to André Breton, having vaguely learnt that he is in disagreement with Eluard, Mr. Vomi du Pinceau hazards an attack on Eluard . . . But never having read Eluard, and not knowing with what Breton reproaches him, the Sergeant of the "King" of Poland, the Rosicrucian Knight, attacks at random, just as he accused Aragon by means of doubtful information. The surrealists know with what to blame Eluard. Let us leave it to them to settle the question in the right time and place.

The Treasury of Errors might be considerably lengthened, but these few samples are enough for the moment.

From an eclectic point of view, the best-documented attempt is that of Mr. Raymond Mortimer, *French Writers and the War*, published in "NEW WRITING AND DAYLIGHT" (Summer 1943). This does not mean that we share the judgments of the author, nor that we approve of his system of classification, necessarily scanty. From the point of view which affects us, the article which we can almost approve is that of Herbert Read, *Au Service de l'Avenir*, which appeared in "LA FRANCE LIBRE" (October 15th, 1943).

It is astounding to measure to what extent writers and artists have allowed themselves to be overwhelmed by isolationism and confused by equivocal propaganda, to what extent they have tolerated the erection of customs barriers between two cultures which used to be so close to each other. How long will it be before we reach an intellectual free trade? In this respect not only are we no more advanced than we were in the XVIII century, we have since beaten a retreat : it is high time that critics, publishers, and above all translators got to work. But this will be a subject for several future articles, and they will have to be written.

Jacques B. BRUNIUS and E. L. T. MESENS.
London, March 1944

LA RIME EN 1940 PAR ARAGON

Drawing by J. B. Brunius

LE REVERS DE SES MEDAILLES
ou DEUX MOTS
AU «CAMARADE» ARAGON

Jadis et naguère . . .
Triste petit vieillard de nadis et jaguère

Tu aimais les audaces
Et les évolutions par bonds
Que mènent à la célébrité
Mais voilà que la bouse te remonte au cerveau

Sois tranquille
L'heure de la récompense approche
Tu seras décoré par la France de Pétain
Où par celle de Gigaulle
Et tu seras académichien
Docteur ès Rimes et fauteuil roulant
Tu seras chanté par Lebrun
Ou bien imposé par Marty
Tu seras déclaré d'utilité publiques
Comme tous les bons endroits
Tu seras fêté à Hambourg
Au cours du même banquet qu' Ilya Ehrenbourg
Tu seras le Gustave Hervé de «Ce Soir»
Ou de n'importe quel autre soir sauf du grand
O! Déroulède des faubourgs.

E. L. T. MESENS.

TWOPENCE. This pamphlet is published by The London Gallery Editions - 23 Downshire Hill - London N.W.3 - for J. Brunius and E. Mesens - and printed by Express Printers - 84a Whitechapel High Street - London E.1

Incendiary Innocence

This 1944 manifesto represents Toni del Renzio's retaliation against Idolatry & Confusion in the sense that he reiterates the propositions of surrealism and suggest the addition of new names to Breton's list of predecessors – such as those of the alchemists and occultists of the past. An attack on Paul Eluard – whose poems E.L.T. Mesens and Roland Penrose had just translated and published (*Poésie et Vérité 1942 – Poetry and Truth 1942*, London Gallery Editions, 1944) – is to be read between the lines of this programmatic text as an appeal for a return to the basic principles laid down by André Breton.

✳

And when I find a mountain rill
I set it in a blaze

LEWIS CARROLL

✳

Behold my Brother, if any one should now come who were willing to
instruct these blockish People in the right way would he be heard ?

The Chemical Marriage of
Christian Rosencreutz
(English edition of 1690)

✳

Je permets à personne, pas même à Elohim de douter de ma sincerité

LAUTRÈAMONT

✳

. . . and in ages of imagination this firm persuasion removed mountains ;
but many are not capable of a firm persuasion of anything.

BLAKE

✳

Je ne m'addresse qu'à des gens capables de m'entendre, et ceux-la me
liront sans danger.

DE SADE

✳

These words are addressed at a time when self-interests slink abroad seeking to exploit the current situation in which ignorance and bigotry, confusion and misrepresentation, weakness and deception, all combine to obscure with the *fog of severed signs* the obstacle that impedes the *actual* process of thought. It is vain to attempt to limit the crisis to the confines of the French tongue. The widespread English and American interest serves to give the lie to that pronouncement. It must, however, be admitted that because the most alive, the most *avant-garde*, poetry in Western consciousness has been recently between the two wars, French, it has naturally appeared to colour the whole question. Clarification if the issues involved can perhaps be achieved by these assertions : firstly that while Aragon appears and is represented as specially French, his collapse is not so, but is of an international character, that is, it is the extreme instance in French literature of a *general failure of nerve* ; secondly and consequently that no solution can be offered by pretending any longer that ' resistance,' in its ephemeral sense, is a substitute for the subtle and informed *resistance of poetry* ; and nevertheless thirdly that today no more than any time is it possible to abstract poetry from the chain of commitments in the ' real world,' in that poetry cannot be recognised but as ir-revocably, of its own nature, tending to transform that world.

These tentatives must be understood to mean that the poet cannot *as poet* be reduced to merely embellishing such political banalities the epigones of Stalin and of Kropotkin may benevol-ently permit. Nevertheless, the efforts to create a ' pure poetry ' will inevitably deny that aim by serving the ugly interests of reaction. In addition, what was reactionary in 1939, is still more so today, that whatever the respect due to the courage and daring of the contributors to EN L'HONNEUR DES POETES, this enterprise serves only to emphasize ' *la honte de la poesie.*' This uneasiness is not quelled by the issue in London of one number of CAHIERS DE LA LIBERATION. More and more the poets in France plunge into the depths of treasonable disregard for *poetry !* Indeed as life itself becomes as cheap and as quickly and easily dispatched as in France today, who can expect the survival of poetic integrity ? Eluard, long ago abandoned by the Surrealists, pitiably drags image after image from his former glory to make some eighty-five lines of nothing new on liberty. In England a similar crop of failure and collapse is visible—Eliot in, say, LITTLE GIDDING, Spender, unable to see ruins before the bombers created them, still to convince us of his 'visions,' the new apocalypse, the new romanticism, the new whatever else is old, outworn or misunderstood, so far has the process obtained in *severing the sign from the signified thing.*

Leaving aside an analysis of the unconscious factors, the most important interbellum intervention into poetry was *automatism.* Though historic forbears may be cited in this, it remains that the Surrealists clearly recognised it for what it was and is, and have never ceased to value it. This has placed Surrealism more or less in sole direction of the vanguard, with the exception of certain differently preoccupied fellow-travellers, of whom de Rougement is a recent and brilliant example. Without passing censure on past or present collaborators of this sort, it can be said that sustained endeavour has been maintained only by the Surrealist movement.

It will not, therefore, be amiss to sum up briefly the present position of Surrealism :

1. Acknowledging Freud's thesis that the unconscious life alone can furnish the valid base for the appraisal of human motives, all conscious justifications seen to float on the surface, Surrealism sees *automatism* not merely as a method of artistic and literary production but as the first visible example of a general reform of methods of knowledge.

2. The fictitious nature of the antinomies at present crippling thought and action must be proved and recognised. This aim is not Surrealism's heritage from the occultists only (what is above is as what is below), but represents a fundamental human aspiration. Surrealism has always tended to that *spiritual plane* whence perception by opposites shall cease.

3. The most ambitious and dangerous of these contradictions to propose to resolve, is that between human and natural necessities Enough however, has been observed of *coincidences* to see chance as *objective*, as a manifestation of extreme natural necessity which finds its way into the unconscious.

4   In certain situations pregnant with danger and repression, the mind seizes upon humour *as a defence*, but paradoxically to such an extent that it passes into *attack*. It becomes the extreme means for the ' me ' to surmount the traumas of exterior reality. This humour has been termed successively ' objective,' ' dramatic,' and finally categorised as ' *humour noir*,' translated perhaps as ' black bile.'

5   These considerations, by the degree of *alienation of sensation* they carry, place Surrealism in a process of occultation, in the struggle in the arena of the ' self,' beneath consciousness, of Eros and the death instincts, which throws into the real world the fatal catastrophes that befall the ' me.' The solution to this conflict—and it entails the solutions to all other contradictions, the rational and the irrational, the dream and real worlds, the high and the low,—constitutes a genuine and intransigeant *intervention into mythic life*, which in the form of a work of art prefigures accurately and in strict order certain *facts* destined to be realised in the real world.

The occupation of this position by Surrealism has directed its attention to the need for a cosmological outlook, the rediscovery of the appetite for universal knowledge. It is not strange, that in facing this problem Surrealism has faced, too, the problem which resides in the *inflation of words* so much more disastrous than the monetary inflation our political leaders seem to fear. More than this, those intellects which could so well attend this evil, have fallen victims to *the general failure of nerve*, the deadly collapse into the confusion resulting from the separation of the symbol from the thing for which it stands. Thus Surrealism cannot consider it enough to present as a poem just a series of pedestrian puns and doubtful jokes*. But apart from this consideration, there is the very important fascination exercised upon us today by the Middle Ages which exist as a beacon of non-humanist lucidity, to which

---

**This must be understood not to reject the delicious humour of Marcel Duchamp which, anyway, is more than mere puns. It is intended to apply especially to the banality of, appropriately, Monsieur* Sous Merde d'Ane. *It is important to point this out as this gentleman has recently insinuated he is a '* poete maudit *!'*

light contributed all the *cursed sciences* with which through the *cursed poetry* Surrealism has an unbroken link.

It cannot be construed as a defeat nor as eclecticism, except by those who lack the enterprise to rise to the demands of history, to affirm today a faith in the dialectic of Heraclitus *and* Hegel, of Eckhardt *and* Engels, of Christian Rosencreutz *and* Leon Trotsky.* Surrealism has been aware of this from its inception but the exigenceis of day-to-day issues have sometimes forced it from prominence ; but in the Second Manifesto of Surrealism the issue is clearly and provocatively stated. Only a deliberate conspiracy has prevented the open statement in this country of the demand for 'the deep and genuine occultation of Surrealism.' Subsequent theoretical texts of Breton and Mabille have developed this demand for ' *hermetic* ' *immersion in metaphysics*, to use a recent phrase of Pierre Mabille. To ensure no misunderstanding of what is being said here, let it be repeated that the occultists, Christian Rosencreutz not the least among them, have supplied Surrealism with the *form* as well as the *content* of some of its boldest and totally recalcitrant assertions, lending them that *furor* of which Agrippa thought to distinguish four kinds. *Furor* is used advisedly of Surrealism, since, as the Second Manifesto has said, it indicates more than a regrouping of words or images, an authentic state of alienation, in fact, definitively freeing the imagination in all the transmutations the *alchemy of the word* can promise.

Alchemy of the verb—released from the limitations Rimbaud had placed upon it—plays a miraculous role in the Surrealist *drama* ; and as psychology becomes more precise upon the nature of the Philosophers so the accuracy with which Breton identified Alchemical and Surrealist researches continues to astound and to confound . Flamel and Lulli have both been listed as Surrealist, while from the former's transcription of the Book of Abraham the Jew has been drawn a description typifying *the* Surrealist picture. The parallelism of these two *révolté* movements separated by several centuries yet intertwined, is most marked in a recent important text, Genesis and Perspective of Surrealism, written by Breton for the catalogue of Art of this Century, where deliberate and conscious references are made to occultists and mystics as Giordano Bruno, Joachim of Flora, Meister Eckhardt, an intimate acquaintance

---

We know less of the owner of the pseudonym " Christian Rosencreutz " than we do of that other, " Comte de Lautrémont," who at any rate we can identify as Isidore Ducasse.

35

with THE CHEMICAL MARRIAGE OF CHRISTIAN ROSENCREUTZ assumed, and the very fount of Alchemy, the SMARAGDINE TABLE OF HERMES TRISMEGISTUS, quoted. This would be alone convincing, without the wealth of that marvellous and exemplary poem, written in Marseilles during 1940, whose title promises sufficiently well its atmosphere and its 'dangerous landscapes' (thank the occultists for this term), the masterpiece, FATA MORGANA. Neither this poem nor that essay, an extremely valuable one, have been cited by those who, emerging from the dark of dusty corridors, cobwebs still in their eyes, now presume to pontificate on and to vulgarise Surrealism and French literature.

When carcases manipulated by *the Devil knows whom* appear on the scene it is clear that 'existence is elsewhere.' This conviction is implemented by the failure to get outside the structure conventional thought has built, of those who most pay lipservice to lucidity and daring. There is the sensitive needle of the dialectic, swinging easily on its fulcrum, instrument fashioned by the most rebellious thought, shunned by those who, unable to reconcile the *gross* material of their being with the promises of the imagination, can face only *reality*, giving to it a sovereignty alien to all ideas of the dignity of thought. What is more and more clear is that *materialism* becomes a weapon only so long as reality, no more and no less than any other perception, is seen to be but a symbol. The attempt to give exclusive value to that reality is but one further instance of the intellectual collapse that resides in the *separation of the sign from the signified thing.**

Vision must return to its pristine clarity, the light which the occultists accord to innocence—an innocence more precisely situated than that mask beneath which ignorance and ill-will have hid themselves—*incendiary innocence* bursting into the flames of the primitive temptations of Bosch. With that innocence returns too, the *capacity for anger*. Authentic anger has been absent from the world. It has appeared only in the violence of a poet like Alfred Jarry whose splendid bile fed its innocence on absinthe. Too long has the pique of psychological short-comings passed itself off as anger, too long the dreary tic of envy as transforming malice . . . It would be idle to particularise and catalogue the list of little men

---

The italicised phrase here, is from Breton. It is interesting to note its similarity of language and outlook with the Schoolmen.

whose pitiful announcements exhaust all meaning from epithets of abuse, and who, for all they intend, succeed only to accuse themselves.

Apart from these men and their dupes, there are others whose pursuit of courses, censured here, has at least been sincere. They, according to their sincerity, will understand this appeal to set about, with all the energy of despair, the urgent tasks facing poetry. Already André Breton, Benjamin Péret, Aimé Césaire, Georges Henein and a number of young French poets are writing poetry which reunites the sign to the signified thing and at last *begins to say something*. They are convinced in their activity by their own and others' theoretical researches, in particular those of Breton, Péret's LA PAROLE EST A PÉRET and Denis de Rougement's LA PART DU DIABLE. The problem of individual and collective love is on the laboratory bench of the poet. When will the poets in English take serious places alongside these French writers in the glory of solving the problems our time has set for us ? Enough of futile discussions, enough of pats on the head and stabs in the back, enough of sneers and stupid snobberies, of reputations for good or for evil, of shocks still in the exhibitionist stage of infantilism, enough . . . how can it be said ?—enough of submission to the ambitions *in this world* of old men—often old before their time—who seek to sit on the shoulders of the poet like the Chimæra of Baudelaire.

Astrologers, poets, seers, stars in the sky, stars in the hand, shiver with the first thrills of innocence when thrown overboard is all we have ceased to regard that might have deterred our sailing. Liberty alone will serve to excite in us the hope that this April we shall see, also, the springtime of revolt.

toni del **renzio**
LAUTREAMONT'S DAY APRIL 4, 1944

❋

Published by
Toni del Renzio, 45a Fairfax Road, W.4
and printed by
The Favil Press Ltd., 152 Kensington Church Street, London, W.8

Declaration of the Surrealist Group
in England

This declaration (here translated into English for the first time) was written by E.L.T. Mesens together with Roland Penrose to feature in the catalogue of the International Surrealist Exhibition at the Galerie Maeght in Paris in June 1947. On that occasion, André Breton had written to Roland Penrose to ask specifically for works by Emmy Bridgwater, Roland Penrose, Conroy Maddox, Robert Baxter, 'Scottie' Wilson, J.B. Brunius, John Banting and E.L.T. Mesens to be sent to Paris for the exhibition. This text represents the last, fruitless effort to reunite the dispersed members of the group.

A danger threatens surrealism nowadays: the almost universal acknowledgement of its importance, an importance which its adversaries hasten to admit, at least implicitly, in the past, so that they can transform it into a catafalque and cover it up with flowers.

We thus feel the need to reaffirm the value and the confidence we give to the surrealist revolution in order to emphasise that we do not consider it as over and done with and to persist to believe in what certain people affect to consider as a 'sin of youth'.

Contrary to the recent tendencies in thought and literature, the International Surrealist Movement has been the only one not to pledge allegiance to politics and sterility in a purely intellectual attitude.

Literature and the arts, under the pretext of making their entrance into the world, have jumped on the bandwagon of the social machinery which lies and leads them where it wants, that is, more often than not, to the privies.

For lack of an analysis which will have to be conducted some day, it is indispensable to us that the situation of the surrealist group in England should be indicated in a few words. The very decentralised structure of English society – which, historically speaking, could be opposed to the extreme concentration in France of administrative or intellectual activities in Paris – has never encouraged the creation of a coherent surrealist group in this country.

The tendencies to irrationality which have always been a feature of English culture, the absence of a coercive logic from the main currents of English thought and even from everyday life, underlines the fact that the Elizabethan dramatists and the Romantic poets hold in the education of children the place which Corneille and Racine hold in France, while nonsense replaces, or at least is added to, fairy tales in their free time. All this throws light on the apparent paradox that this country has given birth to so many precursors of surrealism, from Cyril Tourneur to Swift, Blake, Coleridge and Lewis Carroll, and so few intentional surrealists. One should not underestimate either the particular nature of the Christian moral pressure as is manifested in Protestantism. Far from being confronted with a monolithic adversary like the clearly-defined Catholic church, we are here confronted with an enemy which attacks Man from the inside, an enemy which is itself infinitely divided and superficially liberal. Those are conditions in which the need to form groups in order to fight against oppressive forces is less pressing than elsewhere.

From the beginning of the war onwards, the English surrealist group has experienced some more or less underhand desertions, and has proved to be vulnerable to the attacks of occasional conformism in the months following the war. The most surprising case remains Henry Moore who unexpectedly passed from surrealism to the fabrication of priestly ornaments and sank into the monotonous repetition of shelter sketches, a paltry vulgarisation of his 'reclining figures' before the war. Far from extenuating Moore's case, it is right to add that Herbert Read's eclecticism reaches at present some dumbfounding proportions, that Gascoyne's mystifications leave him prostrate, dribbling at the mouth, and that Jennings has received the Order of the British Empire. It is needless to add to the list the names of persons unknown abroad.

If one compares the various desertions and the rather suspicious vogue for a certain 'genre', a certain artificial surrealist mannerism, enough will have been said on these two aspects of that vulgarisation, the inevitable price to be paid for the success of any innovative enterprise, which one must constantly stigmatise but not give over-importance to.

In England, throughout the war, in spite of the dispersion and lack of contacts between them, some of the signatories of this declaration have never ceased to defend surrealist principles, often from the very midst of reactionary and jingoistic attitudes or in the face of diehard militarism. Notwithstanding limited publishing opportunities and various forms of censorship, they managed to manifest themselves through pamphlets and letters to the press. The pamphlet *Idolatry and Confusion* which exposed as early as 1943 [*sic*; published in 1944] those who profited from underground poetry in France, resulted in the rallying of friends who had lost contact with one another and in the gathering around the two authors of the pamphlet of a fair number of young men and women who were in the military uniform in different countries. This was expressed in *Message from Nowhere* and in the documents brought together later in the anthology *Free Unions Libres*. This was achieved in a spirit of total conciliation, but it also proves that the slightest call for surrealist vigilance finds an echo immediately.

Against the fiercest attacks from outside its ranks and the disintegration of a certain number of its members, the motives of the Surrealist Movement remain totally valid and are at the spearhead of recent events (which cannot be unreservedly said any more of movements of social emancipation). From now on, to change life, to transform the world, to have done with HUMAN MISERY is the task of poetry in action no less than the task of social, even economic, struggle. All around us, people of all sorts are swarming, who have conquered rights to 'leisure activities' but who have lost the secrets of the simplest pleasures and are no longer capable of inventing the delights which modern life has stolen from Man. The Surrealist Movement remains the only one which is concerned with this state of things and the only one which can show a way out of this situation and 'put renewed passion into life' as André Breton suggests in 'Black Light'.

We do unanimously agree on the goals, the means and the criticisms which have been reaffirmed or formulated, during and after the war, by André Breton – in his interview published in *View* (New York), in *Prolegomena to a Third Manifesto of Surrealism, or Not* and in his *Situation of Surrealism Between the Two Wars*, as well as in Benjamin Péret's *Le Déshonneur des Poètes*. We salute the firmness and coherence in action of our two admirable comrades enthusiastically.

Gathered for the first time since the end of the 1939–1945 war, the present members of the Surrealist Group in England adopt the preceding declarations.

John Banting, Robert Baxter, Emmy Bridgwater, F.J. Brown, J.B. Brunius, Feyyaz Fergar, Conroy Maddox, George Melly, Robert Melville, E.L.T. Mesens, Roland Penrose, Edith Rimmington, Philip Sansom, Simon Watson Taylor.

By Way of a Preface

The Inevitability of Surrealism
Thomas Samuel Haile (1909–48)

The following texts are extracted from the as yet unpublished notebooks of Thomas Samuel Haile, a British painter and potter. Written in the late 1930s and early 1940s, the notebooks reveal an extremely acute awareness of the fundamental issues of surrealism and constitute a remarkable theoretical assessment of the basic principles of surrealism by a British artist. Haile's statements mainly relate to painting but also apply perfectly to writing, the two media being of comparable importance for surrealism.

All paintings exist in the 'flesh and blood' in pigment on canvas, in colour rhythms and the representation of forms, in the commonsense reality of the daily press along with other realities such as 'enlightened self-interest', 'the white man's burden' and Guernica. But the painting which discovers us with the explosion of an opening flower has an existence apart from this – an existence in a different reality, of infinite value, compared with the soi-disant realities which would have us buy stream-lined tooth-brushes and mustard-gas. In short, it *is* complete reality [...]

An object has not an nth-dimensional existence independent of the aesthetic consciousness. As the image-N cannot exist without human co-operation, so the object remains in an incomplete three-dimensional reality unless the artist is prepared to approach it in all its dimensions (i.e. 3 + nth) [...] The translation by the artist of aspects of reality, his perception of objects as nth dimensional, is a different process from the mutual approach of his created image-N and the beholder. Both occur in the state of existence we have called the nth dimension but the artist's task is to present with the greatest possible degree of intensity the entire direction of extension of his day in an interpreted form comprehensible to the beholder. The beholder in his life is aware only of the three-dimensional side of reality; the artist, of three-dimensional and nth-dimensional existence. The beholder, via the image-N and the artist, is enabled to contact and to appreciate the whole reality of his environment inadequately realised at first hand [...]

For every object there is a reality of 3 + nth dimensional extension, and it is through the nth that the object and the subconscious approach one another aesthetically. It is also in the 4th state of reality that the subconscious communicates with the subconscious [...]

In the following notes, what Haile has previously called the nth dimension is now called the dimension k-.

[...] The dimension k- is intended to express this special mode of existence [...] A work of art is therefore an aesthetic object or image extended into the dimension k-. Unfortunately, most people approach the rendering of reality, prepared only to receive impressions of the 1st, 2nd or 3rd dimensions [...] If approached on the plane of the dimension k-, the extent to which the rendering exists on this plane, if at all, becomes clear [...] Dimension k- is merely another briefer, and therefore more convenient way of expressing the amount of human passion (as distinct from individual, often conditioned emotions such as fear, joy, eroticism, etc [...]) which has accompanied the conception and execution of the rendering in either of the other dimensions [...]

The artist's aesthetic consciousness intensifies his existence in this extra-state, his conception and execution share this intensified mode of being and the k-image approaching the beholder discovers for him the same intensification [...] The dimension k- is thus a state within a state: it is an intensification brought about by an aesthetic disturbance, of the physical fourth plane in which the human consciousness and external reality find themselves [...] The spectator cannot approach the work of art on the plane of the dimension k- if he is preoccupied with a theory of what the image *ought to* look like or if, for the moment, he is exclusively concerned with his liver; so the culture, thinking only in terms of its foraging, masticating, digesting, voiding and torch-culing, cannot approach the total reality of its existence [...]

Haile's political standpoint is closely in keeping with his aesthetics.

Provided the artist can keep enough freedom to continue his craft, it matters little to him if it is the people's wish to cut each other's throats. Naturally the artist ignores all calls of duty toward such abstractions as Flag, Fatherland and Freedom, for he has two duties only, or rather two aspects of the same duty which is to art, its two facets being the artistic virtue and the propaganda of the message. At the risk of tedium, for the last time is repeated the warning that by propaganda, in this context, is meant not a didactic, calculated effort to make converts [...] but the inevitable propaganda released by the explosion of revealing through the work of art the profound life of the imagination.

On surrealism.

[...] I will say at once that I am convinced that Surrealism is the only proper and valid interpretation of contemporary reality. The k-dimensional location of current phenomena is such that the object makes its profoundest impression, not only on the aesthetic sensibility of the artists, but on the human sub-consciousness of no matter whom. This is the big discovery the contemporary artist has made – his contribution towards a more urgent awareness of reality.

[…] Surrealism has demonstrated by means of the object that the aesthetic sensibility exists within the subconsciousness of all, and is not an attribute apart possessed by a favoured few […]

[…] Surrealism does not confine itself to one craft or even to what are called the arts. It hopes to permeate every human activity […] If a painter can obtain release from his inhibitions, and by letting his entire self converse with life, enrich his craft, so too can the baker and the banker. Surrealism as we see it today is only a beginning, albeit an exciting one. It does not expect to remain stationary and to endlessly repeat its discoveries. By its very nature it is adapted to changing conditions, and as the discoveries of surrealism react on our world, so will the ensuing reality react on surrealism. Surrealism was, and is inevitable.

Poems

Emmy Bridgwater (1906–99)

Except where otherwise stated, these poems were first published, with French translations, in the French scholarly journal *Pleine Marge*, 26 (Paris: Editions Peeters, December 1997).

Closing Time

So comes the flame out of the serpent's mouth
So plucks the bloom, the red-tipped fingered hand.
So, as the clock goes round and round and round
So turns again the record of the sound.

Repeat the space where swallows try their turns
Reveal the place where ants begin to crawl,
Remove the time when rain begins to drip,
Re-seal it all.

Written 1941

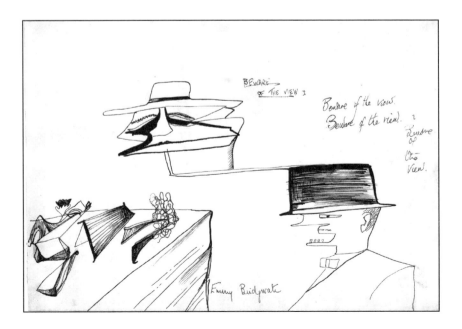

Back to the First Bar

After ten thousand years I will repeat my claim.

Repeat it in the grey garden in the morning when the clouds are swinging and the raindrops are singing and the ground is moist and the worms are turning, are turning the earth that is me.

Little brown bird you will hear

You will take no heed of the insistent whispers, again you will turn to pecking your insect with the striped black body and the blue eyes of a Mona Lisa.

Creeps the penetrating grass over the unvirgin soil, brown as the dried spilt blood.

And again, after the insect,

You will sing

Written 1941

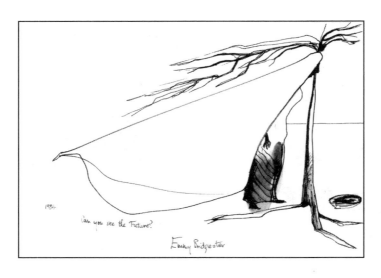

Pigeon Time

The pigeons that circle in the churchyard are crooning
and who is looking with no eyes,
who sees and can't see the pigeons flying round the bombed out grave stones
The tower of the moon is turning, turning blackly into the
searchlights meeting.

What is the starfish doing with his limbs,
and where are all the pettifogging boasters and bankers,
drawing the red line?
In their corinthian pillared banks whispering,
as they lick their fingers to count their bank notes,
Putting a fresh date on the calendar every day.

What is it you have, a pen, a plume?
Oh, I have nothing but an empty coat-hanger,
The grease mark of a head upon a room
Upon the wall of a room that they left three-sided,
and open for all to see the pattern of the wall-paper,
and the place where the fire-place was burning a fire.

Come into the garden, Maud,
throw your crockery into the empty dust-heap,
Break it well, break it, break it into thousands and thousands
Even the excavators will not know, when they are piecing it,
if it were a tea-pot or a jug.

Written 1942

Weed Growing

Come drifting Hairybell that art my pride
Come darkened hand that stirs the porridge pot
Come little links that edge the borderline.
The weeds are growing, slow in growing, quick in dying.

Come to the bordered scollops that distill
        the edge in turning and turning not.
The hot damp air that cries about your throat
        Crying with moth cries, fluttering.

Cock crowing
        child growing
                man dying
                        woman doing

All "A what shall it be then?"
When shall it end and when?
                That is the cry calling in the hot air.
A-stirring of the pot and the hot steam a-twisting a-spiral
Cannot it be a thought
           but
Has it got to be a doing, a done, a finish, an end?

Written c. 1942

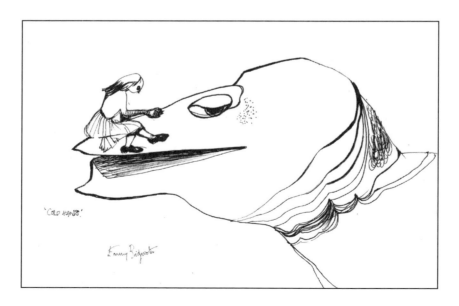

'Cold hands.'

The Journey

Two battered at the Red Lamp hitting the bars.
The shilling dropped darkness forced them up
And they lay sucking the corniced grape along the ceiling.
The corners of the room revolved and swayed
And tree trunks groaned.
Whole passages of time were sliced to pieces
As circling strands of snakes benibbled bits
While grey fish swimming in sawdust, glassy-eyed,
Carved sticky patterns, intricate as sin.
And slow – as the starfish crawls to meet the wave
And slow, but moving as sand in quicksand,
The Chariot arrived…
                              but they were gone.

Written 1942

Storm Trip

Black… murky. Black, black, black and murky night,
That takes away my dreaming making mate
And thunder dropping scissors in the Strand
That cuts the lightning flash I am to take.
I could have made it four weeks to a month.
I am so stupid sitting in the frame.
Well? Is she keeping you from me? Is she, is she?
Am I keeping you from her? She is. I am.

Come take a rake and draw the leaves to where they fall,
Turn back the picture on the winding screen.
It goes. It comes. He takes as the wind drops.
The Sycamore is Oak… the Ash is Bay
And Ivy tendrils twist us as they may.

Written 1942; previously unpublished

The Lost Ones

So many secret passages of night,
are lost there in singing,
So much is heard.
Not a voice,
But an eye and a lip and a turning hand,
a whisper in the blankets.

The swallows were there flying along the telegraph wires,
The kingfishers watching with beady eye and darting at arrogant insects,
The blue broken china my grandmother left in her will,
And darker than black-outs, the picnic table cloth discloses the trampled
                            daisy-chain.
Yes, you can eat my orange, if I can have your knife.

Ring up the curtain on the battlefield,
Boys don't be late.
The audience is waiting to see you,
Meet your fate.

Oh books and thoughts and singing,
and fruit and flowers and you,
"Yes, that's the worst," she said, the old hag,
"Of picking out the handsome ones."

Written 1941

Twisted Centre

Well.   Can you tell me again
Tomorrow and the day after
How many times and how few?
This can't be you again. This can't be you.

Is this the stone that falls in the deep river
Dropping the revolving circle,
Sounding the deep knell
The knell of the deep? Repeat: repeating the sound to sink
To sink in the sound of the grim deep
revolving revolutionary circle;
and weave, wait while they weave the twining threads of gold.
Black into gold will make a red
And red and blue shall make a bed in the centre of a rose.
A Rose. I say it again and we all say "A Rose, a Red Red Rose."

Turn caterpillars into twisted forms
And spit into the street.
The thought you had when yesterday you saw the bowler hatted
American sailor looking at the Marble Arch as if, as if
His mother had given him a clean handkerchief, pressed white and ironed
Without a laundry-mark to tell the time.

Written 1942

Secrets

Despair has taken time and cast a shoe
And dark black rivers circle in the brine
Round pebbles are to rattle rattle down.
"Come, stone him! Stone him!" they cried.
"Reverse… reverse the machine,
make all the black notes red!"

"See that the cheque is crossed," he said,
"Before you turn it inside out."
The footsteps that are coming after
Are after you, after you:
They are feet that are walking in red slippers
In tall black Wellingtons in High Boots.

What is the answer to that?
Repeat: I can't hear what you say.
The line is disengaged, is free.
Come answer then. What is the word you speak
That I can never hear,
Oh Black River?

It is a stranger watching from the corner,
A stranger turning his head and holding his hat in his hand.

When I see his face, I shall know the answer
I shall know the answer to that.
Oh river, river... Come swallow me up –
I shall know the answer.
"Yes," she said, "I can keep a secret."
Little sod. "I never tell," she said.

Whispers are in the laburnum buds, are in
The clustered leaves round the rhododendron,
And pansies are crying for geranium leaves.

Written 1941

The Birds

One

He pulled the blanket over and she drew up the blind. The yellow mice rushed in their corners. The spiders ran behind the pictures. The lecture began on Christ the Forerunner. Only the very young mice sat still to listen. The blackbirds flying near the window passed the word to each other. "Come on! Here we may find something! Something to put our beaks into!" Snap went the windowcord: down came the blind. The birds disappointed, did the best they could. They flew nearer and nearer the window-pane. It was dangerous. It wasn't worth it. But they wanted to get the news – to be the first to know – to pass on the news. What had come to the lecture on Christ? Did one still lie under the blankets? The spiders laughed into their hands to think of the birds outside all twittering and over-anxious.

Two

As she walked into the garden the birds flew down to her pecking at her lips. "Don't do that," she cried. "It's mine. I'm alive you know." "Well, why don't you wear colours?" She heard them talking. "Dead people walk but they don't wear colours. They scream and they talk too." The birds went on chattering about dead people. They all perched up on the holly bush but they did not peck the soft berries. They just stared down at her. All of them stared with their little black beady eyes. They were looking at her red lips.

Three

"Sing a song for the King. Come on, now sing!" The child was shy to start but her mother, standing behind her gave her a little push which startled her into opening her mouth and she began "Wasn't that a dirty dish to set before the King." "Begin again, dear," whispered her mother, "at the first line." "O.K., ma," and she chanted, "Four and twenty Black... oooh," for a peacock had walked in front of her and spread out its tail and croaked "Frico, Frico." The little girl went very white. "Frico, Frico," she said. The birds, who had been sitting on the cornice as part of the decoration, flew down into the court and circled about the heads of the King and Courtiers, fluttering as close as possible. All the people flapped their hands helplessly. Suddenly the little girl pointed at the King. "You must get out of here," she said in a grown-up voice, "This is their Palace."

Written c. 1946; first published in *Free Unions Libres*, 1946

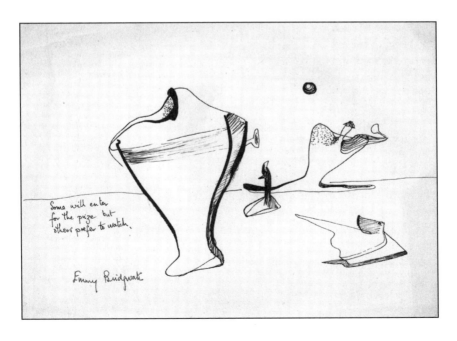

On the Line

Back to the Land
                     To the grape-grown tree.
Red... Red... Full earth Red,
Grown Grass – Grass green growing.

There will be spaces that were stars,
And signing in spaces on the line – signing.
Black death and watered down trees crying
Out shrieking with "It is time,
Now it is time,
And soon there will be no time."
No brushes and no colours and no inks running
No fingers and no hand holding.
The brush not moving in lines
Staying all so staying so will
Eyes looking at all. Eyes always seeing
No rushing waterfall,
No flowering cherry tree.
NO.

Written 1942; previously unpublished

Flowing to the Sea

The purring river rolls
The great cat pounces
And murmurs as it passes by my side
"Am I one cat or many?"
                 I can answer that, "You are all the cats in
                 the world. Exploring, seeking, groping, you search
                 a find to light your eyes and ours. A drift
                 of flowers; a broken twisted twig.

Always in movement you shift a pile of stones,
Leap upon, slide over, creep around and turn circle
And then drip spot by spot to pools and so stay still.

"Yes. You are all the cats in the world."

Then River spoke. "If so, I can be calm or wild.
No tides can rule me. I'll move without the moon
To reach the sea."

Written 1980; previously unpublished

The Symphony

The waters flow swiftly southwards
And on the downwind
There's a startled cry
Some passing bird is stirred to voice its fear
And calling, cries to me, "Remain! Stay there!"
So must I still
But round the avalanche roars
And chasing pebbles drown my waiting feet
And sink them deep below this fearful noise.
The turbulent maze twists on. I am enmeshed
And pain strikes there!
The centre waits… For what?

And now, unheard, the insects stretch their limbs
Clouds driving past disclose revealing light
Cliffs disentangling show some vision that I never
wished to see
And cracking down their sides come trickling streams
That fall in single, placid, liquid drops and slowly
One by One
Their different ways are merged
And unite all in a hymn that ends discordant but agreed
The lake is still.

Then, what's this noise of clattering hands?
Grinding applause?
Yes, I did remain. Here I am.
Four walls are around me.
I waited.
But this is not the same room.

Written 1980; previously unpublished

Over

So helped
By helpless time
The little seconds left.
So few.
And hours and years piled up in mountains
Filled with useless architecture.
Towns,
Broken arches,
Skyscrapers kissing the ground
Mudlicking moments when tears could not drop.
Then water dashed…
striking hard ground
Hiding
In floods so smooth that boats could ride above the
grumbling ground
And never seen, neglected, covered over,
Earth forgotten or recalled
Remaining under the shining surface
Lost
It shall be lost there.

Written 1982; previously unpublished

Jacques B. Brunius (1906–67)

These two poems were published only in French and are translated here for the first time.

Can You See?

Sweet nothing is sweeter
Nothing is sweeter to contemplate than a collapsing church
Can you see the lettuce in the wrecked department stores
The grass grows in the donkey between its frontal lobes
At night banks fill up with dust
Dust of butter dust of flour
Ashes of black horses buried
Under the debris of electrical filing cabinets

Beautiful is a church only when in ruins

The woman dressed in her vest of seeds
Barefooted walking on feet of accountants
Ankle bones
As on candled eggs
Appears sometimes on building sites
To throw the Indian corn of fountains
To harvest the dead wardrobes
To skim the milk of fires
To look under the kernel brambles
For the table of her boredom – kernel – where she carved when young
The name of a very vulgar fish now extinct

Nothing is beautiful nothing is more beautiful when destroyed than a church

Jacques B. Brunius

Naked under the lacquer of pollutions does she run?
Her tunic with star-studding joints
Only Jerome Cardan can see her in the night
But I know her she is the fairy of abandoned arches
She lives on airs on times on keys on vaults
She dresses up in the homage of melancholy soldiers
She sleeps in basins of black water
When the day comes she is Melusine
The little children of Limehouse
The little children of Dorotheenstadt
Bend towards her and drown

And in her Batavian eyes
There shines the provocative splendour mirabelle plum molten lead
Of the sacrificial ogival bombed-out latrines

Published in *Message from Nowhere* (November 1944)

I Love

I love *sliding* I love *turning things upside down*
I love *entering* I love *sighing*
I love *taming furtive hair*
I love *warm* I love *holding*
I love *supple* I love *infernal*
I love *sugar but elastic is the curtain* of *vitrifying* springs
I love *pearl* I love *skin*
I love *tempest* I love *sloe*
I love *seal benevolent* deep-sea *bather*
I love *oval* I love *struggling*
I love *glistening* I love *breaking*
I love *the spark smoking* silk *mouth to mouth vanilla*
I love *blue* I love *known* – knowing
I love *lazy* I love *spherical*
I love *liquid* drums beating *sun if it totters*
I love *on the left* I love *in the fire*
I love *because* I love *at the confines*
I love *for ever several times* only one
I love *freely* I love *namely*
I love *singly* I love *scandalously*
I love *similarly obscurely uniquely* HOPINGLY
I love I will love

Published in *Fulcrum* (July 1944)

62

Ithell Colquhoun (1906–88)

All the following prose poems were later included as integral passages of Ithell Colquhoun's *Goose of Hermogenes* (London: Peter Owen, 1961), an arcane adventure novel based on the alchemical process.

The Moths

I once had two beautiful exotic creatures, one dark, the other excessively blond, called the Crow-moth and the Moon-moth; both were very large.

The Moon-moth was perhaps the more striking in shape – its front wings were so curved as to be almost hooked and the hind wings had long swallow-tails of delicate pink and yellow. The general colour was a pale green, emerald in hue but milky, with borderings and eye-markings of a slightly intenser yellow and an artificial-looking pink. These in their turn were emphasised by a very little deep maroon colour, the only colour of any strength in the design. The wing scales were fine and soft, and long silky hair grew near the body. The antennae were branched and feathery. The flight might be swift, but it must always have in it something of the glide or the flutter.

If the Moon-moth seemed to suggest the vertical, the Crow-moth with its long and narrow fore-wings, stressed the horizontal. It was thick and heavy; its flight, you felt, must be low and darting, though extremely powerful. The fore-wings were sooty black, the veins strongly marked with a powdering of silver scales, each one separately visible; the hind-wings bright yellow with veins and borders of black. Each of the fore-wings looked at by itself might have been a single stiff feather. The body and wire-like antennae were black; I was always a little afraid of the Crow-moth. Did it mean death? And the Moon-moth, those insubstantial cravings after immortality?

Published in the *London Bulletin*, 10 (February 1939)

The Volcano

Right in the middle of the island is a huge volcano, yes, a real volcano, quite as active as Vesuvius or Stromboli – but the islanders are at some pains to keep its activities hidden. They won't even admit its existence to anyone from the mainland. When you see a glow in the night sky and ask them what it is, they will tell you it's a fire in the maquis. So it may be, and very likely the olive trees are burning too; but what has started the conflagration? They won't tell you anything about those seething underground cauldrons that threaten to break through at any moment, and occasionally do so!

What does the pharos say, out there at the end of the jetty? It flashes a message all night through, long after every other lamp is out, but not a message of reassurance. Keep away, it says, I am alight, but so is the mountain! Keep away from these dangerous shores. And from above the inland ranges, I shall be turned into blood, cries the moon; and the stars wide-eyed with terror sink back into their cavernous abyss. Last eruption the mountain burst like a Bank and flung millions of pieces of money high into the air. They were scattered over a wide area of the surrounding hills, and were eagerly searched for and gathered up by the rapacious peasantry. Many a mattress and stocking now bulges with this extraordinary gold. Such was the explosive force that a few coins fell even as far as England. But one never knows what a volcano will do next, so it is best to say nothing about it.

Published in the *London Bulletin*, 17 (15 June 1939)

The Echoing Bruise

I was on the beach; was it a festival, that so many people were about? It must be the day of the sea-sports; my eyes search the holiday crowd for Ildebrando. Shall I recognize him on this dazzling day? There he is! No, it is someone like him. I look in other directions and then suddenly I see him: he is walking with one of his companions, and talking of the contest to come. He is ready for it, wearing his bathing-slip and bonnet. He does not see me.

I am on the cliff-tops; it is getting towards evening, the wind has risen but there are no clouds, huge waves are crashing on the rocks below. Spectators are gathered on the cliff, on the shore, waiting for the chief event of the sports. Here are townspeople and their visitors, with a few rustics from the mountains inland. All at once, a commotion stirs them: Ildebrando comes in sight round the headland, pulling his boat with all his strength against the heavy sea. Will he ever reach the land? Time after time a powerful undertow sweeps him outward. Then putting forth a supreme effort he rides inshore on the back of a ninth wave and is flung beyond the drag of the out-rushing water. He cannot be seen for spray, but a scream of triumph goes up from the watchers. "It has never been done before!" someone tells me in great excitement, "No one else has finished the course. He has pulled all the way from Galva – how many miles? – and in the teeth of a north-east gale!"

"Brando! Branduccio!"

The cries of the people soar higher than the stormy tumult; he has put them above Galva of the grasshoppers, their rival port: Ildebrando is their hero for ever, and even the people of Galva will praise him.

I look down into his boat, rocking now in a sheltered inlet; he has brought from Galva where his sister lives a trophy without price. In the distance and through tears it looks like two little brown dolls, one bigger than the other and lighter in colour; then I see that they are shoes from the feet of his sister's children, his elder sister whose name is future and present and past. Are they made from walnut-shells and the skin of mouse and mole? They prove that his boat has been to Galva; they will always be his greatest treasure.

I look now into the heart of Ildebrando; below the proud surf lie images of the perpetual terror of the earth and sea: first the twelve men he saw frozen stiff in the stranded lifeboat; then more recently the brothers from Lumio drowned in each other's clasp, the one trying to save the other – dragged from translucent depths, so fast were they locked that no one could separate their last embrace and they were buried in the one grave; and finally the corpse he had seen half-eaten by worms at the cemetery – his ribs still echo with the horror of their tawny hue.

Published in the *London Bulletin*, 17 (15 June 1939)

The Double-Village

Do not be misled for a moment: this place is not what at first sight it seems. Do not be deceived by the port, the strand, the square; nor cafés, hotels, cavernous shops, houses gaunt or gay, nor by the churches, soaring or sequestered. The real village is not there. But look inland, up the valley; there you find among cypresses the more persistent counterpart like a reservoir defended by a wall.

Here we believe in giving the dead elbow-room; each tomb is the size of a small house, white or colour-washed, decorated with tracery of iron wire, mouldings, reliefs and unfading flowers made of beads. Over every front door is carved the name of the inhabiting family; this is a very practical idea, because these people never move house. No provision is made for business or pleasure, but only for endurance and contemplation.

They told me that the village had been inundated by an enormous tidal wave and completely submerged. Then I heard that this was not so; there had indeed been a great flood, but the tower was only under water to the height of seventy-six feet. One of the streets too, the one leading to the tower, was still dry; and I seemed to see its tawny colour, the result of centuries of dust. But memory had no part in this picture, for there was no such street or tower in the place I knew.

Published in the *London Bulletin*, 7 (December 1938–January 1939)

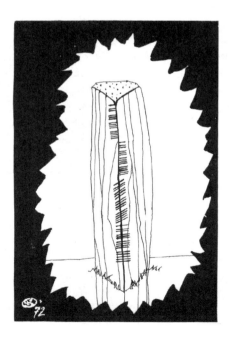

Experiment I

As I was scrambling over the rocky ridges of a valley I came upon a wide fissure slanting down towards the centre of the earth. I looked in and found that its distant floor was water. I began to climb down inside, taking hold of a natural bannister here, stepping on an unhewn stair-tread there, which the uneven surfaces provided. This descent was not easy, as the rock was green with damp and patched with a viscous wine-coloured growth.

I had now penetrated to a vertiginous depth; if I looked upward, the walls rose above me in a cool shaft; turning downward, I could see a cave filled with water the colour of crysolite, illumined from some hidden source and darkened where a turn of wall or jutting rock threw a shadow. One such submerged projection hid the mouth of the cave, making it invisible from the surface of the ground.

I noticed that the water was not tideless, for it began to sink with gurgling sounds, and in its retreat left the cave without light. The rhythm of this tide was very rapid, for scarcely had the cavern been emptied, when the water came lapping back, bringing the light with it. I tasted the water and found it salt; and being unable to explore the cave further because of its swift return, I began to climb back towards the earth's surface. The going was still more difficult than before, as I now discovered fish-like flowers growing directly from the stone without leaves. I could hardly get foot-hold or hand-hold without crushing or gripping these cold petals, which spread their cherry and blue-grey all about the ascent, a salty deposit covering them with a dusty grape-like bloom.

Published in *New Road 1943* (Billericay: Grey Walls Press, 1943)

Experiment III

Another day I was looking for somewhere to live and went in the direction of Maida Vale. From some dingy agent there I got the key of a house to let. Wandering along the streets I came to a road of peeling stucco houses with cat-walks in front and mouldering urns, which could hold nothing, surmounting the plaster gate-posts.

My key fitted the front door of one of these houses; I went in and up the stairs to the first floor. I entered a large room with three windows looking out upon the road; folding doors connected it with the room behind. These I pushed open and found myself in another room exactly like the first; I went over to the central one of its three windows and looked out. Instead of the characterless gardens and hinder façade of a parallel block, I saw a sloping strip of ground overgrown with brambles, then a pebbly shore, and beyond, the crash and smother of Atlantic waves, breaking ceaselessly and without tide. This ocean stretched away to the horizon where it met a misty sky, but did not merge with it – the heaving water set up a melancholy distinction out there; and here within, a briney exultant smell penetrated the panes, cutting through the mustiness of a house long closed.

What extraordinary growths, I wondered, flowered in those wasteful depths? There must be a submerged garden whose silken green held curiosities far surpassing those I had come upon before. Idiots often visit such places and describe what they see; making idiots is one of the sea's favourite games. But when it tires of this from time to time, it casts up instead a supernatural being on an unwelcoming strand, who, ever afterwards, spends his nights asleep at the bottom of some watery gulf.

Published in *New Road 1943* (Billericay: Grey Walls Press, 1943)

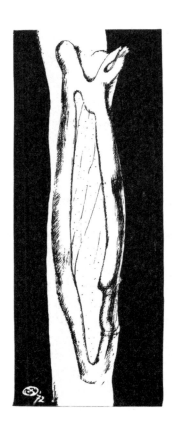

Hugh Sykes Davies (1909–84)

Poem

It doesn't look like a finger it looks like a feather of broken glass
It doesn't look like something to eat it looks like something eaten
It doesn't look like an empty chair it looks like an old woman searching in a
            heap of stones
It doesn't look like a heap of stones it looks like an estuary where the drifting
                    filth is swept to and fro on the tide
It doesn't look like a finger it looks like a feather with broken teeth
The spaces between the stones are made of stone
It doesn't look like a revolver it looks like a convolvulus
It doesn't look like a living convolvulus it looks like a dead one
KEEP YOUR FILTHY HANDS OFF MY FRIENDS USE THEM ON
        YOUR BITCHES OR
YOURSELVES BUT KEEP THEM OFF MY FRIENDS
The faces between the stones are made of bone
It doesn't look like an eye it looks like a bowl of rotten fruit
It doesn't look like my mother in the garden it looks like my father when
                        he came up from the sea covered with shells
                        and tangle
It doesn't look like a feather it looks like a finger with broken wings
It doesn't look like the old woman's mouth it looks like a handful of broken
                    feathers or a revolver buried in cinders
The faces beneath the stones are made of stone
It doesn't look like a broken cup it looks like a cut lip
It doesn't look like yours it looks like mine
BUT IT IS YOURS NOW
SOON IT WILL LOOK LIKE YOURS
AND ANYTHING YOU SEE WILL BE USED AGAINST YOU

Published in the *London Bulletin*, 2 (May 1938)

Poem

In the stump of the old tree, where the heart has rotted out,
there is a hole the length of a man's arm, and a dank pool at the
bottom of it where the rain gathers, and the old leaves turn into
lacy skeletons. But do not put your hand down to see, because

in the stumps of old trees, where the hearts have rotted out,
there are holes the length of a man's arm, and dank pools at the
bottom where the rain gathers and old leaves turn to lace, and the
beak of a dead bird gapes like a trap. But do not put your
hand down to see, because

in the stumps of old trees with rotten hearts, where the rain
gathers and the laced leaves and the dead bird like a trap, there
are holes the length of a man's arm, and in every crevice of the
rotten wood grow weasel's eyes like molluscs, their lids open
and shut with the tide. But do not put your hand down to see, because

in the stumps of old trees where the rain gathers and the
trapped leaves and the beak and the laced weasel's eyes, there are
holes the length of a man's arm, and at the bottom a sodden bible
written in the language of rooks. But do not put your hand down
to see, because

in the stumps of old trees where the hearts have rotted out
there are holes the length of a man's arm where the weasels are
trapped and the letters of the rook language are laced on the
sodden leaves, and at the bottom there is a man's arm. But do
not put your hand down to see, because

in the stumps of old trees where the hearts have rotted out
there are deep holes and dank pools where the rain gathers, and
if ever you put your hand down to see, you can wipe it in the
sharp grass till it bleeds, but you'll never want to eat with
it again.

Published in *Contemporary Poetry and Prose*, 7 (November 1936)

Extracts from *Petron* (London: Dent, 1935)

(Petron, whose adventures we are supposed to know everything about according
to the first chapter of the book, is reawakened from 'the peace of darkness' as he
is lying on 'a swelling bank of violets', by 'a single ray of the setting sun'. Rising, he
walks away.)

Chapter 2

Petron with a merry heart
   passing down the lanes
Makes merry with the signposts;
   A hedger him restrains.

As he went further from the native country, Petron left pasture and came to
arable land. Along the lanes were frequent boards, warning the passer-by of
the penalties of even the slightest deviation from the straight way, 'Beware,'
'Through me men go into a dreadful place,' and such like. These Petron, in an
excess of good spirits, would erase, writing in their place such things as this:

All that you say be my mistrust
Your love all my hate.
Consider well the crows' command
'Nail your soul to the nearest gate.'
Advice is free, and so is land,
The sea knows all about the sand.

While he was doing this, an old hedger came by, and, fearing that the ruin
of the signposts would be attended by all sorts of rural confusion, tried to
deter Petron, telling him that people should know where they go, and why:
that if there were no paths there could be no fields either, and that, for the
most wilful, there could be no wandering from a road which does not exist.
Naturally this argument had no effect, and its obvious justice only served
to irritate Petron, so that he worked ever more industriously on the post,
cutting on its arm a wonderfully distorted picture of the hedger, spelling the
word 'chagrin.'

Perceiving his error, the old man entered on other means of dissuasion.
He fainted. He lay in the road contorted in the most dreadful antics of
epilepsy. He leaned over a gate and vomited blood till the grass was all
matted together: plunged a pointed flint into his forehead: divided each of
his fingers with a pruning-bill into a small hand, and subdivided the fingers
of these again into smaller hands, and so on until he was possessed of many
thousand hands and tens of thousands of fingers. But by all these attempts

71

Petron remained unmoved, depicting them all on the signpost, which grew daily more interesting, and detained an ever-increasing number of onlookers, so that the ordinary business of the countryside suffered serious interruption.

Finally, in desperation, the hedger lay down in the midst of the road, perfectly still, allowing himself to be trampled by the feet of the horses, wheels of carts, wounded by ploughs and harrows as they were taken from one field to another. For three days he remained thus, taking no food, stirring not an inch, and poor Petron was quite nonplussed, for besides that the surface of the signpost was completely covered by the pictures of the hedger's earlier agonies, he was at a loss as to how this new behaviour could be portrayed.

On the fourth day the old man, seeing his advantage, rose again, and having employed his time in deep meditation, at once hit on the means of converting Petron. Taking from his pocket a length of string, he passed it through his head, in at one ear, and out at the other. Then he placed his fingers to his nostrils, and drew the string out from them in the form of a loop, one end in each nostril. The loop he took between his teeth, and leering frightfully for a few moments, suddenly swallowed it, so that the ends of the string which had been dangling from his ears were drawn in and disappeared suddenly and utterly.

Quite terrified, Petron seized his belongings, and fled howling down the lane, never more to meddle with signposts.

Chapter 6

It was quite without malice or intent to wound that Petron, the gentlest of men, happened to step on a toadstool in a meadow. Indeed, it was purely accidental, and for the moment he was not even aware that he had done it, passing on out of the field to a lane. But hardly had he gone a score of paces when he heard a rending groan behind him, and turning his head saw an idiot rising from the earth where the toadstool had been. Once again, poor Petron is involved in a distressing procession, himself walking briskly down the road, the idiot following with curious inarticulate cries. As he moved, his lower jaw, which hung down between his knees, bumped and banged on the road like a loose stick behind a cart, or broken harness on a runaway horse. From time to time he would spit out broken pieces of tooth, and tatters of flesh which the stones tore from his lips and chin. The inside of his mouth was a bright yellow, but soon became maculated with the spattered blood, so that it was of the same colour as the toadstool from which he had sprung.

After a time he seemed to gather his wits, and though he struggled painfully for breath, his cries became more inarticulate, and Petron could distinguish the words of his discourse. He was talking of antiquity, grief, and the antiquity of grief: of memory, pain, and the memory of pain. 'Memory,' he cried, 'memory is a dog that returns to its own vomit. But you, O my persecutor, my fast-trotter, my fleeing foe, you who turn tail but dare not, though your feet itch, break into the downright run of defeat, you call to memory for the stick you have cast, yet when I bring it to you in my teeth, you make off, mistaking my intentions. Little can you know of antiquity, anger, and the antiquity of anger, and how fury displaces kindness in the man misunderstood.'

He shouted all this, with much more of the same kind in its way very good sense, and had the circumstances been different, Petron would have been pleased to stop and hear it. But his alarm increasing every moment, he could not prevent himself from breaking into a brisk run, in spite of the jeers and curses which the idiot heaped upon him. After a while, he had the consolation of hearing the sound of the footsteps and knocking jaw fade into the distance, and when at last the noise ceased altogether, he paused to take breath. Looking back, he saw that the pendent lower jaw had become firmly wedged between two stones by the roadside. The idiot was unable to move on, and in spite of the most violent efforts, unable to speak. As Petron watches, by a series of jerks and contortions, evidently abortive attempts at articulation, the mouth stretches more and more widely, until at last it seems to overspread the whole horizon. At the same time the colours within it, which were rich enough in the first place, undergo a change to still greater brilliancies of gold and red and purple. As this happens, the now monstrous stretch of the jaw restores a certain degree of freedom to the upper part, so that the idiot is able to make sounds. But in place of his former raucous and gasping harangue, there issues from the deepening gloom of his throat and the gorgeous interior of his vast mouth a more melodious utterance, thin piping sounds, warblings, liquid cadences and falls.

Greatly to his relief, Petron sees now that the idiot's mouth is nothing more than the sunset, his throat is the gathering night, and the sounds that issue from it are those of roosting birds, newly-risen nightingales, and owls perched in the tips of his teeth.

Having waited for a time, entranced by the beauties of the sunset, and delighting in the sweet sounds of the evening, Petron passed on towards the sea.

The text that follows is one of Petron's visions which close the book.

Vision VIII

In one of those sandy wastes more often imagined than visited, there lies a plain so rich in a strange vegetation that the traveller stands in wonder on the hill from which he first sees it. For many days his eyes have encountered no shred of green in the barren desert, they have seen nothing more than an occasional shrub, stunted and brown. But now on all sides and as far as the eye can reach the ground is thickly covered with Human Hands, growing from the wrist in the furrowed sand. The fingers are loosely closed, and the thumbs crooked, for it is close on evening time. Soon, as the sun sets, the fingers contract further, gripping the thumb within their clasp, and so they remain through the torrid night, white in the moonlight, a moonlight which can never be described, but which those who have seen it, so they say, can never afterwards forget.

Overcome with astonishment and pleasure at this lovely sight, the traveller takes his seat upon a rock, and gazes over the plain throughout the night. And he is rewarded by the view of a most remarkable phenomenon.

As the first ray of sunlight leaps over the surrounding mountains, a stir passes over the great field of Hands. Each Hand turns slightly towards the sun, while the forefinger stretches until it points directly at his now wholly visible orb. Then, as the sun begins to mount, the forefinger ever following its progress in the heaven, the other fingers uncurl in turn, and the whole hand is outspread in full blossom.

The traveller stays watching still, and sees the Hands turning gently at the wrist follow the movement of the sun all day, erect at noon, declining as the evening comes again, and once again he sees them lying clenched in the white moonlight, the unforgettable moonlight.

In the morning he sees again their strange blooming, but with eyes leaden from want of sleep, and unsteady with thirst and hunger, for both his water and his food were long ago exhausted. Yet he cannot draw his gaze away from the scene before him, and continues so another day. Hardly has he strength enough to await the closing of the hands, and then he too slips to the ground, to die before morning comes again. All about him lie the bones of others who have died in the same manner, white in the moonlight, a moonlight which, they say, once seen can never be forgotten.

The two following texts were found in Hugh Sykes Davies' papers held at St John's College, Cambridge, and are printed here thanks to his daughters, the holders of the estate.

Leaves and Feathers

This is a good game, best played on windy days in autumn. The ideal number of players is one thousand, two hundred and sixty seven, but a good game can be played with smaller numbers, even with none.

The ground should be chosen for its irregularity, and it should be underwater, but not deeply. The ideal depth is one at which the tips of the grass can be seen above the surface, while the nostrils of the players are just below it.

Each player is permitted to raise his nostrils to the surface only when a feather or a leaf has lodged on the tip of a blade of grass near enough for him to have a fair chance of sniffing it in.

Every feather that he sniffs and fails to draw up one or other of his nostrils counts one point against him, and every leaf ten points.

Nothing counts any points for him.

The winner is whoever drowns first, and the loser is the player who drowns last.

Undated; previously unpublished

Loopers

This is one of the best games for single players, for it is considered doubtful, by good judges, whether the pleasure derived from it can be increased substantially, or at all, by having double or treble players. It is, however, quite possible for quadruple players to enjoy it reasonably well, provided that they keep between them a distance of at least twelve miles.

Loops are formed by tying the hands to the feet, or the feet to the hands. Some players find the one easier than the other, some the other easier than the one. Others find the one easier than some, but some prefer one to the other. Left-handed players generally find it harder to do the other than the one, and they can still play a very good game of Loopers by doing some, or even just one. Some one is one Loop or other, and the other Loop is one some. One some is pronounced 'winsome', and it is the winning Loop, unless there is another, or some others.

Any fixed object will do for the centre of the loop, but it should always be unfixed before the game begins, and fastened down again when it is over.

Undated; previously unpublished

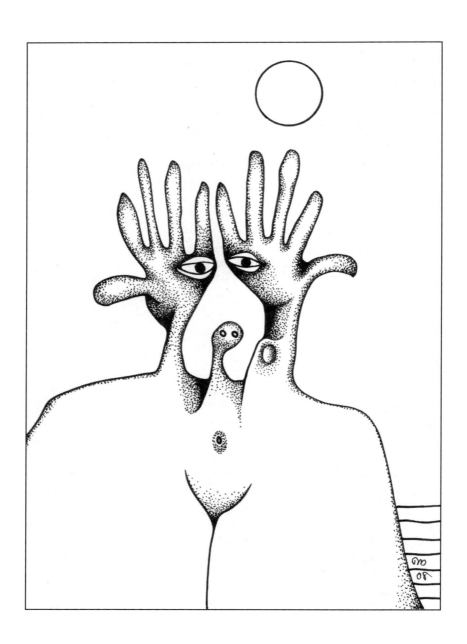

Toni del Renzio (1915–2007)

Can You Change a Shilling?

Who dares to drop the pin destruction of our silence
Who intrudes his shadow across our parallel paths
Who throws his paper wrappings in the wind at our faces
Who is this travel-stained person

Who do you ask these questions
Who do you resent him in the landscape

That man is the image of my father

But you are the image of your father
That man is but your reflection in the clouds of dust
Do you dislike your own image

There is a scratched future
  a pattern of sand and shrubs
  a cracked terracotta figurine
  a dirty reproduction of the Gioconda
  a bad snapshot of your breast (out of focus)
  an antique hat on a chromium stand
  a book of poems by a negro lawyer
  a broken gramophone surrounded by the remnants of a feast and
                            three corpses
  a sewing machine and a sleeping baby
  a glass bowl full of bloodstained water in which some little fish are dying
  a page of typing torn into twentythree pieces
  a rusty sword in a bejewelled scabbard
  a sore of a filthy disease in snow-white bandages

Show me the course you've plotted
Point me the star that guides us
give me the key to the purser's safe

You know the route
The heavens are in your ear
The purser's key fits all the locks
You have the purser's key already
Else how could you penetrate so far

I am the key to all my problems
I am the lord of my desires
I am the prince of pleasures
I am the hunting hound that is chased by the hare
I am the erected tower of instinct
I am the locomotive belching steam and smoke
I am the shadow long at noon and gone at night

Do you know the man who sells dirty postcards
Have you seen the sights of this city
Have you climbed the saint's steps
Will you come to me at midnight

Published in *View*, 3, series 3 (1943)

The following texts are published here for the first time by permission of Pier Luigi del Renzio.

Those Pennies Were Well Spent

It's a far cry from the venus mountain
It's a lost stitch that kills time
It's the strangeness I smell that erects my hopes
           that lays low as with a plague
             those walled cities
           that leads my footsteps across
             the bone-dotted desert of
             ice and hot winds

Do you remember the deserted streets and the solitary steel helmet
The shadows of the statues and the petrified trees
The drawings on the lichened walls the posters of a children play
The beams of the headlamps penetrate the darkest caves
My flaming beacon of your delight reveals the crevices
The rhythms of jazz are good to hear

Here come the tortuous writhings of a tower of steel
The sound of taxis and of sewing machines
The winds of the west stir the perfumes of the east
The fusion, aided by the electric welder, transports us
The telephone in the sandy wastes of night sings songs of the
                    eremite wanderers
The recluses of another age are today the gregarious wanderers
The secrets of my father are at my fingertips
The love that lavished on a wooden box is mine
That love that lay forbidden behind the bars of gold
Those terrible divisions of my father's music
That love is still lavished in the shadows of a tree
But it is not lavished by that flaming sword my father wielded

Today is the first wednesday of the month
Yesterday was the first sunday
And tomorrow the first easter
This is my calendar for the map of you
Goodbye father
Goodmorrow wench from the outstripped limits of my desire
Greetings to you inhabitants of that road leading to the frontiers
The siege has ended the walls collapsed
I could have entered the dark city of inviting pleasure

Can this be me
        this old figure bent and hooped
        this load-bearing coolie
        this portion of stale loaf
        this small piece of torn dirty paper
blown by the wind here and there
sodden with the dew of another dawn
and steaming with the heat of the sun not yet risen
and looking at me

My image is my own eye
It is in your eyes and they are in mine
Can this be that for which men fight
Or is this happiness
Or is it love.

Written 1942; previously unpublished

Untitled

Silence half-chosen and half imposed
tied the tongue
the words knotted on its tip not mine
glib phrases
categories of an alien speech
thoughts evade
the ready-made vocabularies
and bargains
exchange and mart of commonplaces
still unvoiced
the sell-by dates as old as history
countersoiled
hopeworm commerce of unfree trade
price reduced
for everyday impoverishment

From dreams in neglected languages
locutions
mislaid between near and distant pasts
referring
to still unindexed realities
in the mind
fading with the nightly enigma
resonant
meanings too obscure to contemplate
callous signs
the occultation of memory's light
arcane words
structuring a future to be lived
rebuses
mocking monsters of reason awake

Written c. 1970; previously unpublished

St Anne's in Soho

More memory than ruin
No crows call or clack
A figure darts across the road
A book opens itself and reads its fate
What has already started to arrive, in full fig,
The greyish ruins' contrast in full fig
A great east window in full fig
Once daily I stared through plain glass in full fig
A hubbub of grey shadows bustle in full fig
These beings never anything else in full fig
From grey ghosts to still grey memories in full fig
On the corner a heap of splintered plants in full fig
For who can read the signs in full fig
What has happened, happened for each one in full fig
Like stepping through Alice's glass in full fig
Choosing a new order's reason in full fig
New and in order and in unreason in full fig
Among the fractured memories in full fig
The women once I loved in full fig
Rehearsing for one true love I lost in full fig
The love not lost but not now mine
The love that taunts me always
What once I possessed I no longer had
More memory than ruin
The open book recites its tale
A tale of loss and not grasping
What one loves leaves memory behind

Written 12 February 2000; previously unpublished

Untitled

Each memory of each love
Each love of each memory
Each precious fragment
Each aspect of one true love
Pieced together in the magic outline
Which it creates in fragments
All of which fit together remaining fragments
A love anticipated not again reknit
And gone for good
Gone for good yet remaining memory
A lone love not to be destroyed
But having existed perished
Heavy the hand that finished love
And cradled not the gentle aspirations
Against the vulgar invasions

Written 13 February 2000; previously unpublished

EX LIBRIS

TOM DICK & HARRY

Anthony Earnshaw (1924–2001)

These aphorisms come from *Flick Knives and Forks* (Thirsk: Zillah Bell Contemporary Art, 2000), a volume first published by John Lyle's TRANSFORMAcTION Editions (Harpford, Devon, 1981). They are included here by permission of Gail Earnshaw.

from Defeat and Mockery

Gold plated barbed wire for de luxe wars.

Misfortune smiles when bandages turn a cheerful red.

Thanks to heroes, we know how to strike medals.

One of the spoils of battle was a cache of stretchers.

Victorious flags flown too long bleach white in the sun.

Images of love, peace and light thronged the volunteer's nightmare.

That lukewarm anarchist with his banner pink and grey.

Up with stalactites! Down with stalagmites!

Penicillin-tipped arrows.

In our minds we partner God with death. Hospitals, battlegrounds, accident blackspots, trains that jump the metals, air raids… all have their place in the economy of religion.

If all screw threads stripped at the same moment, the world would fall apart.

Accident-prone Dutchmen fear avalanches.

A pair of trousers on their last legs.

A radio station broadcasting secrets for timid nosey-parkers.

from Suicide

Faint-hearted suicides leap off pyramids.

Put the barrel in your mouth. Pull the trigger… You don't have to be a sniper.

The cowardly suicide contrives to shoot himself in the back.

from Damp Days and Brows

Slice open a dogfish and what do you find? Bones!

Gatecrashers and squatters thronged the dock to wave goodbye to the stowaway.

Captured by pirates the ship's carpenter was made to walk his own plank.

The pessimistic seaman passes the time making a liferaft-in-a-bottle.

Don't keep an albatross unless you own an ocean.

A blotting-paper boat.

The millionaire's yacht foundered with all his silk gloves; his hands managed to struggle to the nearest insurance broker.

A lifeboat manned by happy fellows wearing sou'westers set at rakish angles sped to assist the sinking pleasure steamer.

The lifeboat crew pulled for the shore to snatch the beach-yacht's captain from the sandstorm.

Did the Mary Céleste pass the Flying Dutchman in the night?

The fate of the Titanic and her luckless crew and passengers is common knowledge, a footnote to the history of recent times. But what became of the Iceberg?

For the sea an island is a fathomless mystery.

The sea's offshore lakes.

Lakes respect oases as the hermits of their kind.

Rivers suspect oceans of being wild rumours.

The angry bargee slammed the lock gates with a violence that shook the tow path to its foundations.

For the ambitious deckchair attendant, the sand is always whiter beyond the next groyne.

from Too Many Gods Spoil the Manna

Finicky gods scorn warmed-over ambrosia.

Let children play with woolly gods on the Sabbath.

A merry young Jehovah would have used snow, not dust, to form Adam.

Nothing was too good for Noah's passengers. Throughout the voyage they dined at the Captain's Stable.

Whole stretches of the Sea of Galilee remain untrodden by superhuman feet.

Was Jesus the same ichor-group as his Father?

from Kings and Cabbages

The princely game of Musical Thrones.

Bureaucratic inefficiency: the meeting took hours and no minutes.

In lean times, the corner shop greengrocer bites his lettuce sandwich and sighs: "There goes my profit for the week."

from Violent Violets

I know a man who owns a row of railings. He swears they mark the boundary between Right and Wrong.

In Arcadia, stiles over prison walls are a common sight.

"It must be visiting day", quipped the ex-convict as he went through the turnstile to the zoo.

Prison reformers beat thumbscrews into handcuffs.

Did Gilles de Rais notch the hilt of his dagger?

The condemned trapeze artist clung to the wild hope that friendly hands would rig a safety net under the trap door.

"In my youth", reminisced the smash-and-grab raider, "when I was no more than a window-shopper..."

from Work and other Problems

For that spell of time while the eclipse lasted, the miners demanded night-shift rates.

> WARNING
> THIS SLAG-HEAP HAS
> BEEN UNDERMINED
> BY THE WORKING CLASS

A sieve to sort big lathes from small ones.

from **Men**

The misogynist is firm in his belief that the skull-and-crossbones are those of a woman.

The misogynistic gamekeeper sets woman-traps.

from **Women**

Claw varnish for the modern virago.

Most women in Ariadne's sandals would have used the thread to knit a saucy hat.

from **Sleep**

The lazy insomniac cannot be bothered to go to bed.

Insomniacs should play nursemaids to somnambulists.

The energetic sleepwalker goes to bed with a rucksack strapped to his back.

from **Mumbo Jumbo**

Catholic cannibals eat mermaid on Fridays.

Thirsty dervishes drink at the nearest whirlpool.

That squinting cyclops!

Pegasus, once a foal? Once a fledgeling?

from **The Ideal World**

With prosaic Life taken into custody
and Poetry triumphant
these edicts will be fulfilled
and the world made perfect

+ All submarines shall be crewed by ex-miners.
+ A truce shall be called between teeth and food.
+ A glut of wheels shall be manufactured to provide cheap travel for all.
+ All surgical gloves shall be punctured, irreparably.
+ Waterfalls, tears and dew shall speak the same language.
+ The KKK shall tar and feather only on black and snowy nights.
+ Every motorway shall have a gutter with an old man selling matches.
+ Surveyors shall give the "thumbs down" to dowsers.
+ Cuckoos shall only lay in nests built in clumps of mistletoe.
+ Astronomers shall publish papers cluttered with asterisks.
+ All dining tables shall be set with...Flick Knives and Forks.

David Gascoyne (1915–2001)

All the texts reproduced here were written in 1936 or 1937. Most of them first appeared in *Man's Life is This Meat* (London: Parton Press, 1936) and were later included in Gascoyne's *Collected Poems* (Oxford: Oxford University Press, 1988). The others, as indicated, are here published for the first time. Many of these texts were unearthed from the British Library archives thanks to the patience and perseverance of Roger Scott, the indefatigable and undisputed specialist on the life and work of David Gascoyne.

And the Seventh Dream is the Dream of Isis

Research suggests that the following text is the first English surrealist poem ever published. It was proposed by 17-year-old David Gascoyne to Geoffrey Grigson, the editor of *New Verse*, one of the few English avant-garde magazines to welcome surrealism. Grigson published it in no. 5 (October 1933).

I

white curtains of infinite fatigue
dominating the starborn heritage of the colonies of St Francis
white curtains of tortured destinies
inheriting the calamities of the plagues of the desert
encourage the waistlines of women to expand
and the eyes of men to enlarge like pocket-cameras
teach children to sin at the age of five
to cut out the eyes of their sisters with nail-scissors
to run into the streets and offer themselves to unfrocked priests
teach insects to invade the deathbeds of rich spinsters
and to engrave the foreheads of their footmen with purple signs
for the year is open the year is complete
the year is full of unforeseen happenings
and the time of earthquakes is at hand

today is the day when the streets are full of hearses
and when women cover their ring fingers with pieces of silk
when the doors fall off their hinges in ruined cathedrals
when hosts of white birds fly across the ocean from america
and make their nests in the trees of public gardens
the pavements of cities are covered with needles
the reservoirs are full of human hair
fumes of sulphur envelop the houses of ill-fame
out of which bloodred lilies appear.

across the square where crowds are dying in thousands
a man is walking a tightrope covered with moths

2

there is an explosion of geraniums in the ballroom of the hotel
there is an extremely unpleasant odour of decaying meat
arising from the depetalled flower growing out of her ear
her arms are like pieces of sandpaper
or wings of leprous birds in taxis
and when she sings her hair stands on end
and lights itself with a million little lamps like glow-worms
you must always write the last two letters of her christian name
upside down with a blue pencil

she was standing at the window clothed only in a ribbon
she was burning the eyes of snails in a candle
she was eating the excrement of dogs and horses
she was writing a letter to the president of france

3

the edges of leaves must be examined through microscopes
in order to see the stains made by dying flies
at the other end of the tube is a woman bathing her husband
and a box of newspapers covered with handwriting
when an angel writes the word TOBACCO across the sky
the sea becomes covered with patches of dandruff
the trunks of trees burst open to release streams of milk
little girls stick photographs of genitals to the windows of their homes
prayerbooks in churches open themselves at the death service
and virgins cover their parents' beds with tealeaves
there is an extraordinary epidemic of tuberculosis in yorkshire
where medical dictionaries are banned from the public libraries
and salt turns a pale violet colour every day at seven o'clock

when the hearts of troubadours unfold like soaked mattresses
when the leaven of the gruesome slum-visitors
and the wings of private airplanes look like shoeleather
shoeleather on which pentagrams have been drawn
shoeleather covered with vomitings of hedgehogs
shoeleather used for decorating wedding-cakes
and the gums of queens like glass marbles
queens whose wrists are chained to the walls of houses
and whose fingernails are covered with little drawings of flowers
we rejoice to receive the blessing of criminals
and we illuminate the roofs of convents when they are hung
we look through a telescope on which the lord's prayer has been written
and we see an old woman making a scarecrow
on a mountain near a village in the middle of spain
we see an elephant killing a stag-beetle
by letting hot tears fall onto the small of its back
we see a large cocoa-tin full of shapeless lumps of wax
there is a horrible dentist walking out of a ship's funnel
and leaving behind him footsteps which make noises
on account of his accent he was discharged from the sanatorium
and sent to examine the methods of cannibals
so that wreaths of passion-flowers were floating in the darkness
giving terrible illnesses to the possessors of pistols
so that large quantities of rats disguised as pigeons
were sold to various customers from neighbouring towns
who were adepts at painting gothic letters on screens
and at tying up parcels with pieces of grass
we told them to cut off the buttons on their trousers
but they swore in our faces and took off their shoes
whereupon the whole place was stifled with vast clouds of smoke
and with theatres and eggshells and droppings of eagles
and the drums of the hospitals were broken like glass
and glass were the faces in the last looking-glass.

Published in *New Verse*, 5 (October 1933)

The Symptomatic World

I

Following an arrow
To the boundaries of sense-confusion
Like the crooked flight of a bird
The glass-lidded coffins are full of light
They displace the earth like the weight of stones
Eating and ravaging the earth like moths
Which follow the arrow
In a shower of freshly variegated sparkles
Confusing the issue of the arrow's flight
Till its feathers are all worn out
And the trees are all on fire
The pillow-case is bursting
The feathers are blown across the roofs
The room is falling from the window
And O where did that woman come from
Who chases the muleteer across the pampas
And covers her flaming face with the huge shadow of her hands?

II

The pinecone falls from the sailor's sleeve
The latchkey turns in the lock
And the light is broken
By the angry shadow of the knave of spades
Kneeling to dig in the sand with his coal-black hands
His hair is a kite to fly in the dangerous winds
That come from the central sea
He is searching for buried anvils
For the lost lamps of Syracuse
And behind him stands
The spectre whose lips are frozen
Unwinding the threads of her heart
From their luminous spool
She is stone and mortar
And tar and feather
Her errand is often obscure
But she comes to sit down in the glow of the rocks
She comes with a star in her mouth
And her words
Are rock-crystal molten by thunder
Meteors crushed by the birds.

III

Intelligence resides in the sparrow's beak
And the seat of the will is the wing of the wasp
I am here I am there and my mind is in the middle
I hold in my hands the knob of the door of sleep
I stand on my feet on the rock of the principle
And my eyes are on top of my head
They see all that happens in the sky
The horse that bears his master in his mouth
And is ridden by the girl with red plush breasts
My ears grow out of my feet
And they hear all the sounds under ground
The ringing of bells in the caves
And the whisper of wandering roots
The intellect resides in the mineral's neck
And the seat of the soul is the mouth of the stone
Which is why the earth's veins are so stopped up with sand
And the sea is so full of green flame
For the earth is a kiss on the mouth of the sky
And the sky is a fan in the hand of the sun.

IV

This is my world this is your realm of clay
Our dreams have all come true
The ash of sleep is deeper than dust on the stairs
Of this mine-shaft brimmed with gold
The sunken garden of a fugitive
Cold with black rain that stains the soil like ink
Enigma like a skull with petrol eyes
A sprouting head of plumes of silver grass
That haunts the sanded paths
The booming caves are full of birds
With silken wings and beaks of solid stone
Who pass the time away
With burning feathers from their tails
In the flaming waterfall
This is my world this is your garden gate
Our vistas stretch a thousand leagues from here
As far as the forests full of moving trees
As far as fingers holding tigers' skins
As far as bushes on the window-sill
As far as castles with unlicensed towers
As far as caskets full of human hair
As far as clouds on fire and dying swans
On lakes that swallow beds as fast as tigers swallow hands.

V

On the sidewalks of New York
There are women who pass to and fro with napkins wrapped round their heads
So that no one can see their eyes
And machines lean out of the windows to record the number of their footsteps
A record is made of the sound of falling coins
That cover the streets with silver and cause fruit to ripen in bowls
And the lift-boys chant:
The sea comes once too often up the street
And the wind goes once too seldom down the sky
And their song goes on till morning
When the inhabitants put logs outside their doors
For the children to make fires in all the gutters
Which awakens the town to the sound of derailed trains
While baskets of boot-buttons light up the distant hills.

VI

Undoubtedly the sun has burnt his hands
Undoubtedly the corn has grown too high
And when this is done
The first-class trains will stop running every afternoon at five o'clock
And the passengers next morning will alight
In a ditch of frozen milk
Their thoughts will return with regret to their twice-locked trunks
Full of borrowed dresses and discarded wedding-rings
They will groan with dismay at the thought of the coming day
Full of empty bags and crumbs of stalest bread
From house to house the frost will spread its warnings
And weathercocks fall from the roofs.

VII

The needle glitters inch by inch
And the sound of its stitches reaches the sea
Where bombs explode in every other wave
And the beaches are paler than curd
I return there every other night
Wearing the same clothes, breathing the same air
And the weasels only laugh at me but it is not my fault
I can hardly help it if the lines of the meridian resemble fish
That fly away
To where the heat softens the equator
With hair growing out of its ears
And birds' nests in its hair to keep the rain off
The rain that whispers in decrepit castles
Great clots of clay and the effigies falling to dust
Preserve us from the singing towers
And the chapter which turns the page of its own accord
For fear of reading its own history there.

Published in *Contemporary Poetry and Prose*, 6 (October 1936) and 7 (November 1936); *Collected Poems* (1988). The *Collected Poems* includes an additional stanza at the beginning of the poem. However, since Gascoyne himself published this poem in an erratic and fragmentary way I have chosen not to include that additional stanza as part of the poem here.

The End is Near the Beginning

Yes you have said enough for the time being
There will be plenty of lace later on
Plenty of electric wool
And you will forget the eglantine
Growing around the edge of the green lake
And if you forget the colour of my hands
You will remember the wheels of the chair
In which the wax figure resembling you sat

Several men are standing on the pier
Unloading the sea
The device on the trolley says MOTHER'S MEAT
Which means *Until the end.*

Written c. 1936; published in *Man's Life is This Meat* (1936); *Collected Poems* (1988)

Direct Response

The four elements are sitting at the table
There is a shipwreck on the sands
A warm hand in the mist
Flowers turn colour in the mist
Without moving

Sensitive needles at the extremity of breathing
What can you etch upon the eyes' quick web?
Up to your middle in the dewy grass
Whose profile can you sketch upon their filmy screen?

I have long forgotten why I am young
A bird's blue shadow trembles on my breasts
A bird's song blossoms from the water
Till my neck bends back in a curve like stone
And I am neither white nor warm nor cold

Written 1936; published in *Man's Life is This Meat* (1936); *Collected Poems* (1988)

Lost Wisdom

In the first morning
A cry above the unborn roofs
Of solitude and pain
A faint odour of vegetable matter
Fringing the violet lids of night
And hanging from the water's eyes
The simulacrum of the damned

Disturbance in the weather makes me see
The little angels without wings
The brittle needles in the sand
The ropy veins of polypi
And all the seamless seams

And now and then
From every abandoned mouth
An unstanched stream must flow
And then as now
The graves were opened once
And gold was melted by the snow
Like lilies sown in sifted stone
And gathered once for all.

Written c. 1936; published in *Man's Life is This Meat* (1936); *Collected Poems* (1988)

Reflected Vehemence

Umbilically detached, of sorrowful mien and at the same time decked out in cobwebs – these vanquished ones, whose breathings propagate violence and fear. Their padded fingers point uselessly to the stars of their own eloquence. It is just the same as ever in the outgrown pavilions of vegetable matter. As though St Valentine had smudged the last letters of a secret pact with the powdered antennae of a forgotten fly. As though flying itself were only circular.

But here where the graphite byways meet, there is bound to be always fresh water. See how the ruched waterfalls reply with shaking heads to the invitations of the warrior-like foliage. They seem to vanish in thin air, gasping for a more fluid means of expression. The tinkling belfries glide away of their own volition. Eggs break during the fencing lesson. Masonry, tightly clasped to the nape of the ritual, buries itself in an indulgently frothing explosion of the head, whereby the closed gates are breathed upon anew by the breezes of loyalty and honour. Thus clouds are born.

In my hand lies the same whispering, nail-headed dude, ever imploring the benefice of a hippograph.

Written c. 1936; published in *Man's Life is This Meat* (1936); *Collected Poems* (1988)

Charity Week

To Max Ernst

Have presented the lion with medals of mud
One for each day of the week
One for each beast in this sombre menagerie
Shipwrecked among the clouds
Shattered by the violently closed eyelids

Garments of the seminary
Worn by the nocturnal expedition
By all the chimeras
Climbing in at the window

With lice in their hair
Noughts in their crosses
Ice in their eyes

Hysteria upon the staircase
Hair torn out by the roots
Lace handkerchiefs torn to shreds
And stained by tears of blood
Their fragments strewn upon the waters

These are the phenomena of zero
Invisible men on the pavement
Spittle in the yellow grass
The distant roar of disaster
And the great bursting womb of desire.

Published in *Man's Life is This Meat* (1936); *Collected Poems* (1988)

The Very Image

To René Magritte

An image of my grandmother
her head appearing upside-down upon a cloud
the cloud transfixed on the steeple
of a deserted railway station
far away

An image of an aqueduct
with a dead crow hanging from the first arch
a modern-style chair from the second
a fir tree lodged in the third
and the whole scene sprinkled with snow

An image of the piano tuner
with a basket of prawns on his shoulder
and a firescreen under his arm
his moustache made of clay-clotted twigs
and his cheeks daubed with wine

An image of an aeroplane
the propellor is rashers of bacon
the wings are of reinforced lard
the tail is made of paperclips
the pilot is a wasp

An image of the painter
with his left hand in a bucket
and his right hand stroking a cat
as he lies in bed
with a stone beneath his head

And all these images
and many others
are arranged like waxworks
in model birdcages
about six inches high.

Written 1936; published in *Collected Poems* (1988)

The Cubical Domes

Indeed indeed it is growing very sultry
The Indian feather pots are scrambling out of the room
The slow voice of the tobacconist is like a circle
Drawn on the floor in chalk and containing ants
And indeed there is a shoe upon the table
And indeed it is as regular as clockwork
Demonstrating the variability of the weather
Or denying the existence of man altogether
For after all why should love resemble a cushion
Why should the stumbling-block float up towards the ceiling
And in our attic it is always said
That this is a sombre country the wettest place on earth
And then there is the problem of living to be considered
With its vast pink parachutes full of underdone mutton
Its tableaux of the archbishops dressed in their underwear
Have you ever paused to consider why grass is green
Yes greener at least it is said than the man in the moon
Which is why
The linen of flat countries basks in the tropical sun
And the light of the stars is attracted by transparent flowers
And at last is forgotten by both man and beast
By helmet and capstan and mesmerised nun
For the bounds of my kingdom are truly unknown
And its factories work all night long
Producing the strongest canonical wastepaper-baskets
And ant-eaters' skiing-shoes
Which follow the glistening murders as far as the pond
And then light a magnificent bonfire of old rusty nails
And indeed they are paid by the state for their crimes
There is room for them all in the conjuror's musical-box
There is still enough room for even the hardest of faces
For faces are needed to stick on the emperor's walls
To roll down the stairs like a party of seafaring christians
Whose hearts are on fire in the snow.

Written 1936; published in *Collected Poems* (1988)

The Rites of Hysteria

In the midst of the flickering sonorous islands
The islands with liquid gullets full of mistletoe-suffering
Where untold truths are hidden in fibrous baskets
And the cold mist of decayed psychologies stifles the sun
An arrow hastening through the zone of basaltic honey
An arrow choked by suppressed fidgetings and smokey spasms
An arrow with lips of cheese was caught by a floating hair

The perfumed lenses whose tongues were tied up with wire
The boxes of tears and the bicycles coated with stains
Swam out of their false-bottomed nests into clouds of dismay
Where the gleams and the moth-bitten monsters the puddles of soot
And a half-strangled gibbet all cut off an archangel's wings
The flatfooted heart of a memory opened its solitary eye
Till the freak in the showcase was smothered in mucus and sweat

A cluster of insane massacres turns green upon the highroad
Green as the nadir of a mystery in the closet of a dream
And a wild growth of lascivious pamphlets became a beehive
The afternoon scrambles like an asylum out of its hovel
The afternoon swallows a bucketful of chemical sorrows
And the owners of rubber pitchforks bake all their illusions
In an oven of dirty globes and weedgrown stupors

Now the beckoning nudity of diseases putrifies the saloon
The severed limbs of the galaxy wriggle like chambermaids
The sewing-machine on the pillar condenses the windmill's halo
Which poisoned the last infanta by placing a tooth in her ear
When the creeping groans of the cellar's anemone vanished
The nightmare spun on the roof a chain-armour of handcuffs
And the ashtray balanced a ribbon upon a syringe

An opaque whisper flies across the forest
Shaking its trailing sleeves like a steaming spook
Till the icicle stabs at the breast with the bleeding nipple
And bristling pot-hooks slit open the garden's fan
In the midst of the flickering sonorous hemlocks
A screen of hysteria blots out the folded hemlocks
And feathery eyelids conceal the volcano's mouth.

Published in *Man's Life is This Meat* (1936); *Collected Poems* (1988)

Competition

The ultimate perfection of wisdom is undesirable
And more so especially since the tongue-twister started to reign
And the calloused trestles proclaimed their destinations
And over the whole of Utopia there was a thick white blanket
Which muffled the horrible sound of colliding trains
And out of the national rivers came swarms of bees
Which mumbled inaudible fragments of ancient lore
Hurrying past the surrounding palace of water
Which stood on its feet to wave them a last good-bye
When the door of the closet opened
Disclosing an endless vista of swollen gems
Turning incessantly upon their pinprick navels
Displaying their undersides to the curious eyes of the thieves
Their lambskin vests to the fatuous undertakers
And all their embroidered fins to the end of the world
So the captain said this has nothing to do with the earthquake
This is awfully brave of the woman I'll give her a bone
And turned in his bed which was folded in half down the middle
And covered with pieces of eight
And announced to the night that a prize would be given for beauty
And another for wearing a wig.

Written 1936; published in *Contemporary Poetry and Prose*, 1 (May 1936)

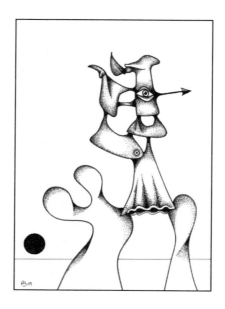

Untitled

Today there is fur on the tongue of the wakening light
There is dust in the darkening streets
Whose tongue is brick dissolved in lime
The sound of sight
Reduced to ashes by the height of the bloom's decay
In the caverns of the smell
Where moth-balls leap like mole-hills in the pocket of grey fowls
Thin grey fowls with leather gullets
and with claws of too much rain
Too much anthracite in pain
In the cities of the plain
Although anthrax is the secret of the way to find your way
From the paling of the pillars to the breaking of the bars
Where the breezy bellows stand in bright array
And the castanets are forming little holes in women's sleeves
In order to allow their sound to breathe.

Written 1936; previously unpublished

Untitled

Sickness and charity like death's heads tied to the mast
Return to the bottomless sea from whence they came
Where islands of snow sink like holes into the heart
And the revenge of death is remembered no more
By those whom the firmament betrayed
Life's nebulous champagne is forgotten before it is drunk
For each of its bubbles is a brief lapse of its blood
Of the somnolent clay whose arms embrace the sleeper
And whose veins are of lead – life's bouquet
Has lost all its scent for those who plucked it
Their senses are tied to the battlecry's torn floating web
And the landscape's oblivious light is
Where islands of snow sink like holes into the heart.

Written 1936; previously unpublished

Untitled

The gradual emergence of the
Instincts the hard sharp
Laughter of the sudden daylight
And out of the sleepy funnel
Of the waking mouth
Breath
Merges again with the waiting
Whiteness of what is to be.

Written 1936; previously unpublished

Salvador Dali

The face of the precipice is black with lovers;
The sun above them is a bag of nails; the spring's
First rivers hide among their hair.
Goliath plunges his hand into the poisoned well
And bows his head and feels my feet walk through his brain.
The children chasing butterflies turn round and see him there
With his hand in the well and my body growing from his head,
And are afraid. They drop their nets and walk into the wall like smoke.

The smooth plain with its mirrors listens to the cliff
Like a basilisk eating flowers.
And the children, lost in the shadows of the catacombs,
Call to the mirrors for help:
'Strong-bow of salt, cutlass of memory,
Write on my map the name of every river.'

A flock of banners fight their way through the telescoped forest
And fly away like birds towards the sound of roasting meat.
Sand falls into the boiling rivers through the telescopes' mouths
And forms clear drops of acid with petals of whirling flame.
Heraldic animals wade through the asphyxia of planets,
Butterflies burst from their skins and grow long tongues like plants,
The plants play games with a suit of mail like a cloud.

Mirrors write Goliath's name upon my forehead,
While the children are killed in the smoke of the catacombs
And lovers float down the cliff like rain.

Published in *Man's Life is This Meat* (1936); *Collected Poems* (1988)

from Automatic Writing

The chafing streams of nickel in the skull are mute to the glory of the arctic sleeping-draught's no longer silent tension and the ilex is in bloom. Pieces of air detach themselves from other pieces of the air in which the stench of summer has awakened the moist freesias and covered the glistening moss at the volcano's summit with fresh eggs. Up the chimney flies the unhappy sponge and lays its head upon a plate of steel, where no amount of purification has been able to unfasten the abandoned crates from their smokey resting-places in the hollow of a tree. Full of the smoke of lotus and of thrusted elbows, whose emanations resemble the thin lips of the chilly vase's laughter. From roof to roof its ankles grow, until they cannot constitute a danger to the monocles of the dangling crabs which impede our progress from room to room. [...]

A candle is snoring in the sky above the house with many rooms; its flame is like a flag above the roof. A cabbage rolls along the path which leads up to the door, and a bird had just flown into the top room of the house, a four-leaved clover stamped upon its back. This is where our pilgrimage ends. We have drunk our own flesh and we have gazed out at the fur, and now our path leads us out of the treacherous world into a house full of rooms whose altitude it is beyond our power to measure. Dark horses stamp their powerful hoofs beneath the bedroom floors, the loam of batteries is quick with electric shocks. Nothing can break the spell of the Atlantic breakers which are surging in the leaden cupboards where the quick and the dead have left their garments to decay beneath the unauthorized gaze of a colossus with heels of gold. In either hand he holds a bird with broken wings, in either eye there turns the oar which ploughed the winter sea when the boat had sunk into the sands. In either eye, that is to say, the hand of chance beats time instead of dancing to it, and the shoes of time beat chasms through the floor [...]

Published in *Man's Life is This Meat* (1936); *Collected Poems* (1988)

from The Great Day
(Simulation of Paranoia: Acute Mania, Delirium of Interpretation,
Delusions of Grandeur)

When I woke up it was indeed very beautiful. The bannisters were shining intensely and the stairs were coming up towards me. I was well aware that my eyes were no longer clinkers. I sat on the edge of the bed with my feet in the sand and watched the ambulances going past the window. What carnage, what thunderbolts and, indeed, what pascal lambs!

But I'm afraid you will hardly believe me when I tell you that at the hour when the night-bird should have flown, at the hour when all the matrons no longer able to have children should have entered the room, precisely at the hour of the one-o'clock séances and balloon-course meetings, it was one o'clock. I went out as the cock was crowing and held my head above the basin which I thought was full of water but it was full of cream and ashes. This, of course, brought on one of my fainting fits, but I soon recovered, and there, to my infinite surprise, sitting on the left-hand flap of the little linoleum wigwam which looks like a forge-bellows, was she upon whom my heart had been set ever since that marvellous sunset long long years ago when my heart was still a captive beating its pitiful wings in the great silence of all the empty rooms and the dining-rooms and the cellars and all the wine-cellars. Without a moment's hesitation I went straight up to her and caught hold of her icy hand, I can tell you, and her mouth was like a beautiful garden full of flowers and full of bronze flowers and beautiful flowers like medals. My adoration knew no bounds and the sound of my kisses on the air was like the flapping of sheets, I know what I am saying, it was like the bottling of new wine. But what was my amazement and despair when she told me she could never be mine for she was married to a leper, imagine it, what could I do to prevent my heart from bursting into a million little pieces like diamonds and emeralds and rubies, yes real ones, not imitation glass ones, never, I have never stooped to that. She tore her hands and feet away and a great pain shot through me like a shaking spear, for it was she who had taught me all those wonderful words, it was she whose blood I had wanted to feel pulsing beneath mine own, and now she refused to open her veins for me! My passion was so frightful that I might have spat right in her face, but fortunately I was able to restrain myself and she passed away like the great wave after the earthquake of Messalina. [...]

And then it was at last time for the operation. Were I to describe to you all the details of what took place on that memorable occasion it would take me ten times as many books as there are stars in the universe and in any case my pen would have turned to dust long before I got to the last astonishing page where I should sign my name in letters of flame and of gold and in letters of flaming gold.

First of all it was like **drinking oxygen**. I had the gentle maternal pigeon on the one side of me and the symbol of the crossed keys on the other, so I felt perfectly safe. It was like looking at that picture of a girl climbing a rope which hangs on the wall in the warden's room, it was like woollen buttons and angel's skin. It kept changing all the time, of course, so that one minute you saw the pattern of the minutes coming and going and the next you saw the sort of sawdust that they throw down on the floor if you look at it hard enough. I stretched out my hands and they went sliding far away out over the multitudinous seas whose voices came to me like the sound of chariots and firearms roaring and terrible chariots grinding the limbs of the helpless Christians to powder. Then the bed started to go up and down but it wasn't a bed it was a sort of automatic pianola and it began to gallop away with me on its back right into the middle of the forest where the chimneys were all smoking away like fury because the silly things thought it was the middle of the night. But I knew better, of course, so I sat up there and then and told them that I wasn't going to stand any more of it and I smote the ridiculous creature with the wooden leg across the backside, and they were absolutely terrified of my voice like hundreds of railways thundering and my face like a red-indian's. But what am I saying? They thought they could scratch me with their tigers' claws and their eagles' talons, the wretches, they thought they could scratch my eyes out, but they weren't going to get away with it so easily. I lifted my imperious iron hand, I whose hands and feet are the very seal of all that is powerful and triumphant in this miserable world where the flowers only grow to please me, I lifted my iron hand and it became a sword and sceptre against all the wicked and unruly tongues that were clacking in the caverns in the valley of the shadow of death. My breathing became like the wind of the great tempest and I felt my body growing to stupendous size and the blinding light was like organs playing. What noble pity surged into my melting soul and how I knew everything that had been forgotten down the centuries by the mages and the saviours and the nobility of all European countries! For that was easily the greatest moment of all, when all the candles were being burnt for me and all the banquets were being given in my honour and all the assembled nations were singing songs in which my name was mentioned at least once, I think I might even say without boasting that it was mentioned ten times, in every verse.

After that, as you will well understand, it was not so difficult for me to come back into the daylight. The room was just the same as before except that the window seemed to have lost something of its original transparency and the table had been replaced by a milk-float. Nobody seemed to notice any particular change in my appearance, but if they had looked closely enough they could not have helped seeing the little snow-white footprints on my eyelids and the little black stars on my lips. In any case I took no notice of them, for I despise all men who have not the words LOVE AND DEATH inscribed on their banners, and when I went out in the evening I met my mother walking in the garden. She was wearing one of my most cherished hats and I told her of all my recent experiences, ending up by explaining how I had been awarded the Nobel Peace Prize for my exploits among the red-skins. She smiled gently and, lifting her veil, began to talk about the time she went to tea with Georges Sand. Then we went to choose the flowers for the wreath. And the phosphorescent night began to fall.

Published in *Janus*, 1.1 (January 1936)

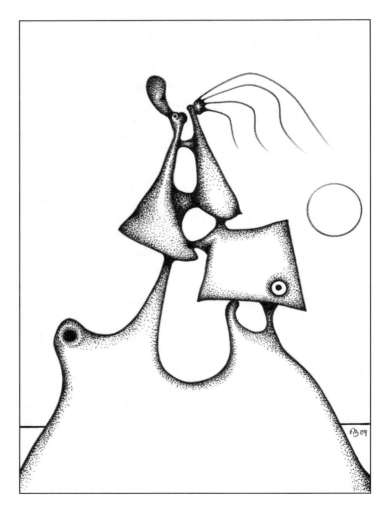

Humphrey Jennings (1907–50)

Except where otherwise stated, the prose texts reproduced here were published in *Contemporary Poetry and Prose* in June and September 1936.

from Three Reports

The conditions for this race, the most important of the Classic races for three-year-old fillies, were ideal, for the weather was fine and cool. About one o'clock the Aurora again appeared over the hills in a south direction presenting a brilliant mass of light. Once again Captain Allison made a perfect start, for the field was sent away well for the first time that they approached the tapes. It was always evident that the most attenuated light of the Aurora sensibly dimmed the stars, like a thin veil drawn over them. We frequently listened for any sound preceding this phenomenon, but never heard any.

Written 1935

The Funeral of a Nobleman

This nobleman's career may be likened to a wintry sun, which shines between storms and sets suddenly in gloom.

The apartment in which he expired is distinguished by an awning in front of the window.

It was a delightful sunny day. The enthusiasm was immense. At Parkside the engines stopped to take water. Mr. Huskisson having got down from his carriage, the Duke beckoned him to his side and they were just shaking hands when a cry went up from the horrified spectators who perceived that the body was that of Lord Byron being carried to Newstead. Reason never recovered from the hideous coincidence. The journey was completed amidst a deluge of hostile rain and thunder, missiles being hurled at the coach in which the Duke was riding.

From the tomb seawards may be seen Brighton afar off, Worthing nearer, and closer in, in the valley, the village of Salvington.

Written 1936

from Reports

The front windows on the ground floor were entirely closed with inside shutters and the premises appeared as if altogether deserted. In a minute the front door was opened and Mr. Kellerman presented himself.   His manner was extremely polite and graceful. His complexion was deeply sallow and his eyes large, black and rolling. He conducted me into a parlour with a window looking backward, and having locked the door and put the key in his pocket he desired me to be seated. The floor was covered with retorts, crucibles, alembics, bottles in various sizes, intermingled with old books piled one upon another.   In a corner, somewhat shaded from the light, I beheld two heads, and entertained no doubt that among other fancies he was engaged in remaking the brazen speaking head of Roger Bacon and Albertus.

Written 1935

When the horse is impassioned with love, desire or appetite, he shows his teeth, twinkles his coloured eyes, and seems to laugh.

He shows them also when he is angry and would bite; and volumes of smoke come from his ears.

He sometimes puts his tongue out to lick.   His mouth consists of the two rays of the eternal twins, cool as a sea breeze.

Written 1936

Two American Poems

The hills are like the open downs of England – the peaceful herds upon the glassy slopes, the broken sea-washed cliffs, the beach with ever-tumbling surf, the wrecks that strew the shore in pitiful reminder, the crisp air from the sea, the long superb stretch of blue waters – the Graveyard.

> As we journey up the valley
> Of the Connecticut
> The swift thought of the locomotive
> Recovers the old footprints.

Written 1938; published in the *London Bulletin*, 12 (15 March 1939)

Report on the Industrial Revolution

The material transformer of the world had just been born. It was trotted out in its skeleton, to the music of a mineral train from the black country, with heart and lungs and muscles exposed to view in complex hideosity. It once ranged wild in the marshy forests of the Netherlands, where the electrical phenomenon and the pale blue eyes connected it with apparitions, demons, wizards and divinities.

Written 1936

Prose Poem

As the sun declined the snow at our feet reflected the most delicate peach-blossom.

As it sank the peaks to the right assumed more definite, darker and more gigantic forms.

The hat was over the forehead, the mouth and chin buried in the brown velvet collar of the greatcoat. I looked at him wondering if my grandfather's eyes had been like those.

While the luminary was vanishing the horizon glowed like copper from a smelting furnace.

When it had disappeared the ragged edges of the mist shone like the inequalities of a volcano.

Down goes the window and out go the old gentleman's head and shoulders, and there they stay for I suppose nearly nine minutes.

Such a sight, such a chaos of elemental and artificial lights I never saw nor expect to see. In some pictures I have recognised similar effects. Such as *The Fleeting Hues of Ice* and *The Fire* which we fear to touch.

Written 1937; published in the *London Bulletin*, 1 (May 1938)

I See London

I see London
I see the dome of Saint Paul's like the forehead of
Darwin
I see London stretching away North and North-East,
along dockside roads and balloon-haunted allotments
Where the black plumes of the horses precede and
the white helmets of the rescue-squad follow.
I see London
I see the grey waters of Thames, like a loving nurse,
unchanged, unruffled, flooding between bridges and
washing up wharf steps – an endlessly flowing eternity
that smooths away the sorrow of beautiful churches –
the pains of time – the wrecks of artistry along her divine
banks – to whom the strongest towers are but a moment's
mark and the deepest-cleaving bomb an untold regret.

II
I see London at night.
I look up in the moon and see the visible moving
vapour-trails of invisible night-fliers.
I see a luminous glow beyond Covent Garden
I see in mind's eye the statue of Charles the First
riding in double darkness of night and corrugated iron
On the corrugated iron I see wreaths of fresh flowers
I see the black-helmeted night and the blue-helmeted morning
I see the rise of the red-helmeted sun
And at last, at the end of Gerrard Street, I see the
white-helmeted day, like a rescue man, searching out of
the bottomless dust the secrets of another life.

Written March–April 1941; published in *Humphrey Jennings*, ed. Mary-Lou Jennings
(London: The British Film Institute in association with Riverside Studios, 1982)

I Saw Harlequin

I saw Harlequin dancing by the factory chimneys
    Lay your head low on my arm love
And his name was Chartism
    Close your eyes and rest
I saw Harlequin stepping through the machine-shops
    Hold your breath and wait
I saw Harlequin peeping in the fox-holes of Kharkov
    Hold your hand tight in mine
And his name was the Russian guerilla
    Open your eyes and watch
I saw Harlequin marching to the Curzon Line
    Raise your head high in the light love
And his name was the Red Army
    Open your eyes and cry
I saw Harlequin waltzing in the cornfields
    Lay your head low on my arm love
And his name was the true people
    Close your eyes and dream

Written 1943; published in *Humphrey Jennings*, ed. Mary-Lou Jennings (London: The British Film Institute in association with Riverside Studios, 1982)

Sheila Legge (1909?–48?)

I Have Done My Best for You

And there appeared unto me a woman with chains upon her wrists riding on a bicycle; and in her hand a banner bearing these words: THERE ARE NO MORE WHORES IN BABYLON.

"Look," she cried, "There is the Queen Mary setting out on her maiden voyage."

And indeed it was an impressive sight, out there in the desert, that tall ship built entirely of the most costly marble (for no expense had been spared) setting out on her maiden voyage with her cargo of candles and all her passengers climbing up the gangway, which was made out of point de Venise and had been lent by the Pope, with their clothes and their medicine bottles neatly packed in rooks' nests and a ham sandwich for the journey.

But I could not really give my full attention to the spectacle, diverting as it was, for I was already late so, bidding her farewell, I went on alone. Seeing that I was in earnest this time she pedalled away in the opposite direction, leaving me in total darkness. I took out the packet of needles which had never left my side since I waved good-bye to my mother only that morning at Liverpool Street Station and, as I had expected, the largest needle of all gave out a phosphorescent glow sufficient to cast a beam of light on my path. (You can imagine how careful I was to keep an eye on it and the relief I felt when the sun rose, six minutes later).

Tea was over long ago when I arrived, but Mogador had left a note on the table to say he would be back shortly so I sat down to wait. But when the wax-figures who had left their showcases because it was half-time began to melt I realised that the house was on fire and there was nothing to be done. Everyone showed great signs of agitation and my calm was vastly envied.

"Oh dear," they moaned, "If only there had been a flood. We could easily have made ourselves boats out of all the chamois leather gloves in the garden and there would have been no danger."

However, it was only another FALSE ALARM. The icecreams on the table, who had been most undecided as to their chances of survival and would have hoisted the white flag long ago but for my sangfroid, quickly refroze themselves into even more spectacular shapes than before and all was ready for the feast. All, that is, except myself for by now I was more than tired of so many interruptions, so, pushing my chair back, I lay down on the floor and fell asleep.

And on the third day I rose again and sold my wife for thirty pieces of camembert and my infant daughter for three francs fifty.

Published in *Contemporary Poetry and Prose*, 8 (December 1936)

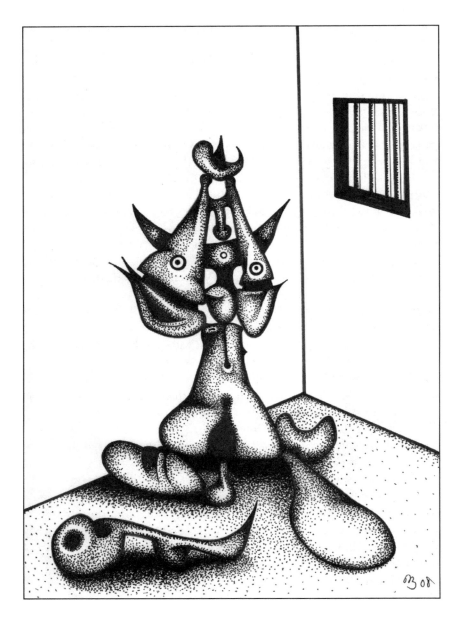

Len Lye (1901–80)

Knife Apple Sheer Brush

Take a	knife
To an	apple
The pith lies	sheer
With the mind take a	brush
Peel the skin of your own	pith
See the sinews of	feeling
Traced in the glow of vegetable	dyes
Pinioned by the black	action
Of the cadmium	sun

HAYTER

Effigies seen in the name of Hayter
Twang echoes into ritual

For YOU of HIM
In gamut of aesthetic

With cat gut to a violin
As boots floor walls to his painting

WHO on this floor of a gallery
Self-lured to savour hypnotic mind juice

Lick the cat chops of experience
Where mind stands confronted with mind

Not by museum label or institution
But by the work of one man

Seeking responsibility for his version
Of the transparent skin of the universe

Revealing unique and priceless scarecrows
Guarding the seeds of experience

Acrid dyed flamboyant and confident they stand
Vital as those of exhumed cultures

They state the primitive faith in eternity
In colors of life and death

Such living candescent signs
We ignite now to show

Some luminous version of the future
From ourselves long ago

Published in *Tiger's Eye*, New York, 7 (March 1948)

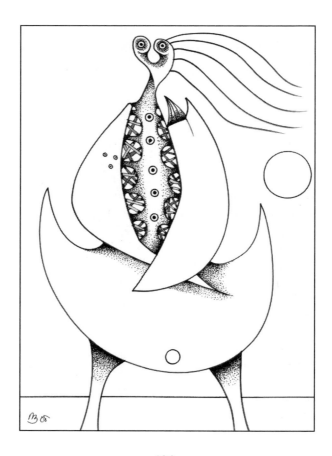

from Song Time Stuff

Chair in Your Hair

Painting painting where is thy mind sting: there there under the chair: not *under* the chair says poppa Cézanne in the legs of the chair says poppa Cézanne: that old chair? Chair in your hair Cézanne Cézanne. A chair in the mind is worth none in the bush. A chair is a chair so leave it there.

Dazing Daylight

Out of the dim paleface past a continual daylight mind has given us an alibi for reality. The age old eye check double check on surroundings to ease our doubts. So now reality you don't bogey us we bogey you with a ten out of ten tag everytime. All's set in the world with a visual chamber in broad dazing daylight.

My Merely Me

Naming the père not choosing a godfather but hoping you realize he rationalized his chiselled images of realism into painted shavings of excellence the Joseph to his Mary incidentally he presented to painting the very first sensible theory that painting had mentally evolved up to then.

I am mere Len Lye with my own rationalization antagonistic to all theory and all painting up to now with buckets of sense more Lennie than Lyzze. The less theory with optic the more eye truth in the psyche the better.

I Parent My Thesis

Parenthesisly the finer subtleties of first causes one and all were sifted and eventually will be when perspective points vanish.

As it was ever was and shall be the material of the first limbo's gambol starting from the sprang of some early mould workings on the was of corrugated age surfaces smooth for water hencing on to the original blood structure.

Such structure has a slant on the inner structure of all material things in spite of puzzlebrow: don't you think.

Published in *Life and Letters Today*, 18.11 (Spring 1938)

Conroy Maddox (1912–2005)

For John Welson

The well-oiled engine of the lawn-mower
Rumbles desirously in a landscape enclosed by walls.
The sweet song of a pure voiced girl
Tells of obscenities, of money, of death without repose;
The teeth of a comb embedded in the brain emit so pleasing a sound
                    when struck.
From the canvas arises a stench of half-decayed meat
Languorously inviting us to roll in it;
The pincers from a fairground machine
Pick over limbs with a disgusting meticulousness,
Steel scissors piercing the side gleam smooth to a caressing touch.
Neither set-square nor ruler are useful
When a liner dragged by a bicycle enters through a crack –
Under the jaundiced gaze of a giraffe, a flower blooms.

Written October 1978; published in Silvano Levy, *Conroy Maddox: Surreal Enigmas*
(Keele: Keele University Press, 1995)

The Playgrounds of Salpetriere

In the rancid hearts of tropical forests are the long neglected playgrounds of Salpetriere, the illustrated journals of your childhood, the horizon of your difficult reality and human sentiments, where the light of the paraffin lamp only occasionally penetrates the hour that determines your presence and illuminates the miraculous invisible obstacles of your incertitude. An image of exquisite anonymity, of imperturbable contradictions, an image so uncertain that it seems to forever tremble between the believable and the unbelievable and phantom-like questions the validity of all that surrounds you.

The taps give off only a few drops of ink; infidelity stains the wall. Tomorrow like yesterday has passed thus, and only the scarecrow talks eloquently, will talk at all. You have everywhere surpassed yourself in naivete yet you are less than the funereal iris that registers the changing seasons, the imperfect and hovering faces of the seasons. I have observed your voice which is a musical box awaiting the winds direction that it may sing its loving denial of love. Like the sea-crabs the red and white flowers of the coarse landscape are not protected by their colour, and those that have survived remain unknown. Your flight was thought to be the riddle of the birds' migration since it was you who fashioned freedom, who dreamed exclusively of yourself dreaming.

Written 1940; first published in *Surrealism in Britain in the Thirties*, exhibition catalogue (Leeds: Leeds City Art Gallery, 1986)

Poem

I seek only the gestures of a lonely ruthless quest.
To resurrect if only for a day the marvellous
dressed corpse of my desire.
Larvae, moths, necrophors.
To perpetuate the cemetery, to plaster you with sea-weed,
to open up a gap and produce a breakdown.
Everything that goes up comes down.
Across the wailing of a frightened child
an orchestra is playing Brahms, and a mutilated dog
is wiping itself on a copy of night.
If I fail to stab you in the back
it is because the dancing woman is irritating.
The weight of silver the uselessness of gold.
I am not here to dispel illusion,
I who love the darkness alive with fear
and death that crawls with black lips.
There was a beginning which I cannot remember
and an end which I have lost sight of,
for I have domesticated the nightmare.

Written 1941; first published in *Surrealism in England: 1936 and After*, exhibition
catalogue (Canterbury: Herbert Read Gallery, 1986)

For He Was Only a Worker

He would lie on the wings of black swans
Like a breast shaped antennae
Imitating a scented landlord
He would dress the glaciers with sand storms
And play with the dust clouds of sleeping chimeras
He would cover the priests with spittle
All leering and lice
All bones and bowels
He would paint "aux barricades" on the batons of the police
And break the clocks head with cinders
In palm decorated taxis of amber
In VIOLENT ACTION
But he was only a worker
And did as he was told.

Written 1939; previously unpublished

Another Day

If the air is crumbling to ashes
and offal is riding a tramcar
is it because the fish-eyed priests are
laughing
as he stuffs the dull-faced madonna with mould.

Written 1939; previously unpublished

For Robert Melville

You spoke of the sea-anemones
and the days of unattainable water
on the sharp points of fur.
You dangle trophies of hallucinating mystery
and bare your chest for devouring,
where the walls have ears
and the shadows are well polished.
Your face is an erotic domain,
the property of specialists.
Your face is a tree,
no its a cage of emerald insects.
Your face is a minutely detailed anecdote.
Your face is a chain.
Its not a chain its a carcase,
its not a carcase its a glass breast,
its not a glass breast its a swamp,
its not a swamp its a woman waving,
its a vast desert, its a strangled child
its a book, no, its a black olive.
In any case its the property of specialists.

Written c. 1944; first published in Silvano Levy, *Conroy Maddox: Surreal Enigmas* (Keele: Keele University Press, 1995)

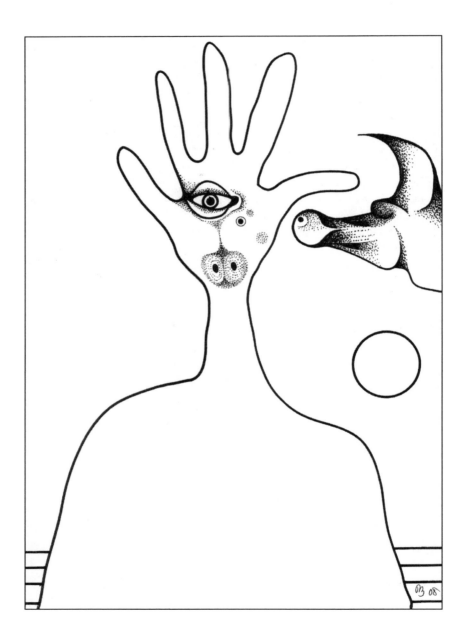

Reuben Mednikoff (1906–76)

The following text is taken from typed notes found in the Tate Archives, London.

The Secret that is Eternal No More

Here is the source, the secret, the rhythm…life.
The long breath, the short breath, and then the pause.

The long breath that would discover, that would seek to know.
The short breath that, now knowing, would taste and drink in delight…
And then the pause – the in-dwelling – the moment that is contemplation

Again the long breath that, knowing, would seek for more…
And the short breath that, having sought, would seek the moment that
              is the dwelling upon the moment known…
And then again the pause…and that is knowledge.

And within is the inner beat that shall lead to the knowing of joy.
The beat that wells up within as the fountain of knowledge and life
              pours slowly in upon you.
The beat that swells the knowing of life.
The beat that lifts the moment of knowing, more quickly, to
              the rhythm that is the ultimate joy.
The beat that tempers the moment of joy, soon to be known.
And then again a pause that, with knowing, which is without
              fear, is a longer measure…endless perhaps…
              the endless moment that can contemplate the
              coming of full being.
Then, at last, the pulsing and throbbing that marks the moment
              that is beyond knowing…beyond contemplation…
              and the culmination of joy.
This, the last, is birth and death-to-darkness and the secret that
              is, eternally so, no more.

Written 8 August 1935; previously unpublished

The two following texts were first published in *Sluice Gates of the Mind: The Collaborative Work of Pailthorpe and Mednikoff*, exhibition catalogue (Leeds: Leeds Museums and Galleries, 1998).

August 4, 1935

(spoken during analysis of *Flashing Lights*)

Flashing lights…drops of blood.
Severed heads…torso bespattered with blood…
wretchedly loathsome…loathsome in its torture.
Angered because of nipples bespattered with nipples of blood.
Nipples are drops of blood. Each breast is a tortured thing,
with a nipple of blood. Savaged…torn by child…
Bitten by child for sap…for milky blood.
Wretchedly loathsome with milky blood.
Beads are water…limpid body…no…that is wrong…
A curtain of glittering blood beads dripping a purple garment.
Heed no blood that reveals the tortured deed or thought.

August 7, 1935

(while re-shaping *Flashing Lights*)

Flashing lights…drops of blood.
Drops of blood…drops of flashing light…
Singing nipples, singing drops of blood…
Singing drops of light…singing, singing.
Drops of life…singing drops of life…
Drops that dropping sing delight…in life.
Dropped in torture…sung in nurture…
Dropped delight.
Drops…drops…drops…in night.

Poem

Give me the terpsichord for wild and gentle music
Give me the ladled harp – the mountainous lilt that meddles not.

Flowing like the brook, with gentle curvature, the leaping flageolettes drip
like molten drops of green and violet mellifluence.

What devilry? What heights?
Low cunning likens not the drawn sword with the flatulent breathing of
heaven-sent geometricians.

Drinking babes heave no greater sighs. White liquids flow no smoother; are
tipped no quicker to the petulant lift of flower-like hands.

Rocked melodies gain no greater sweetness.
Darkness hides no sweeter flowing.
Yet would the wooden mallet or the hate-heavy iron fall with more
vicious-heavy anger than the unexpected heaving of that gentle and mild-
seeming child?

Darkness gave no greater crime to this world and light revealed no greater
innocence than shone from those gleaming innocents, those eyes, that
mocked the evidence which flurried hands and hearts pit-a-patted.

Written 1937; first published in *Surrealist Objects and Poems*, exhibition catalogue
(London: The London Gallery, November 1937)

The following texts have been selected from the documents deposited after Med-
nikoff's death at the Archives of the National Galleries of Scotland. They are
reproduced here as written and published with the permission of the Estate of
Reuben Mednikoff. I am grateful to Ann Simpson, Curator of the Archives, National
Galleries of Scotland.

Untitled

Lift the palsied arm and grovel the earthborne into amnestied fury
Grivel the thrust into amnestied furtherance
Pulse the puling pips into the anthrax of pujoram. Est is.
So lacking the positive dissociation from pulolam istimcide
He jawed the jist of jetsam into piebald pills that hurried the high hatted
hicks on to pusilanilous
Linx et noir

Dienometerox est probonismulem
Est hiejorax
So it is

Vow no lived sweat on pin-cushioned heavy-omsts
Let live, live and so add vital pubis est vainglorum
Snip the potato crisp in twain and plant tomatoes, not in vain
Sim sam supper in train – vain add glorium
Thrust the knocking knees to fly-ing to perjoryam
Est is
Sling the seed, flick the cracker and like the seedling
                    into flappering earth-trowelled land et is adperforam.

Written 1948; the manuscript is annotated "'Garrick", Port Isaac, Cornwall, 1948'

Untitled

Down the clustered glade the mobile corpse trotted to tarry only for a cock-leg against a devastated tree. Preferring those that lay athwart a boggy hole. Two massive heels and a clawry eye summed the nobility of his stock and then no summer came to repair the ravages of the slime that would, of course, endlessly disturb the caricature of the limes.
No story. No game. No nostalgic origin could help the iron will of his toe. Then lead no man to mercy. Led the leading lights of inaptitude.

Glad was I of this faint hope. No summer fog to hide this wintry tale. No corpse. No stink.
Then I can hope to favour the sod that clutters heavy from the spode.
Did terror strike? Did darkness filter through the sieve of day and muster pestilential spots to the cloak of wisdom-hidden inaptitude?
Dare the daughter of the Nile. Dare the Saturnalian hierarchy. Sickness swells my stomach to the ends of tubes and fear catacombs my bowels.
Dark holes, hovel the intestinal malnutrition and avaricious tendencies end at the grout.

Written 1948; the manuscript is annotated '"Garrick", Port Isaac, Cornwall, 1948'

The following text, as its title clearly implies, was written after one of the seances organised by Mednikoff and Pailthorpe while they were living in Cornwall.

Cornish Seance

The Spirits move in less than time denotes a care,
                 and rhapsodies fly skelter to the winds,
                 unheard by Thrall or Drone.
Does the high-noted wanderings of thin and slack
                 lean nearer the aphrodisiac?

Soul and harmony linger in union
         and frightened faces lean from scraggy loins
Thus do the high, multifarious whinnyings
         and deleterious mutterings
         suffer the caking clog of more noises and puffs.

Droll and lean the filtering lights
         in the moon's irradiant shadows
         and more and more the whirl of cadences
         roar their tottering notes.

Droll and lean the harboured reverence
         of many picketed murmurings
         lean in the upper bedroom windows
         droll in the thrust and scurry of the moon's strange wind.

Written c. 1948. Signed Richard Pailthorpe: see glossary

George Melly (1926–2007)

Mabel's Dream

I

A thousand horse-faced poets
Wearily project themselves into the past.
They walk clumsily
Among the moustaches and straw hats.
They listen
For the creaking of an ingenious machine,
Or try to remove a lemon
From the wrong tree.

One, who has no chin,
Hastens to incriminate his mistress,
Who has no hair,
Slobbers disgustingly over a minute shell,
Which has no lips,
Pretends that he has a bird in his head.

The sight of so much stupidity provokes me to considerable anger.
I am going to attack the lot of them with my shooting stick.

II

The two silent figures by the enormous excavations
Are unable to escape.
My sister has entrapped the four of them
In her hair.

The gun is always surrounded by corpses.
The eggs by birds.
The bicycle by lovers.

We are going to ascend in this ornate balloon
Much to the astonishment of the ladies and gents.

Published in *Free Unions Libres* (1946)

Poem

If your brains
     were wool
You could not knit a sock

If your brains
     were thread
You could not manipulate a sewing machine

If your brains
     were dynamite
You could not blow off the top of your head.

Published in *Free Unions Libres* (1946)

On the Occasion of a Birthday

Despite those who turn their coats as often as they light a cigarette
Your friends become your enemies
As soon as they buy a bowler hat
The umbrella of your integrity protects you perfectly well
From the rain of medals and honours which causes the heads of so many
To sprout with unbelievably vile fungi
     E for the Elephant of Celebes
     L for love without frontiers
     T for the torch of black humour
     E.L.T. MESENS my friend.

Published in the catalogue accompanying the E.L.T. Mesens exhibition at Galerie Isy Brachot, Brussels, 1970

E.L.T. Mesens (1903–71)

All the texts that follow were published during Mesens' stay in London from late 1937 onwards, when he acted as Director of the London Gallery and 'leader' of the Surrealist Group in England. They were published in the bilingual volume of poems *Troisième Front/Third Front* (London: London Gallery Editions, 1944). The translations into English were by Mesens himself, with the assistance of Roland Penrose.

War Poem

To André Breton

I was born the twenty-seventh of November nineteen hundred and three
Without god without master without king
AND WITHOUT RIGHTS

> *As far as the eye can see*
> *Human human misery*
> *As far as the eye can see*
> *At random roofs and houses*
> *As far as the eye can see*
> *Lingering trailing robes*
> *Acadungemy*
> *League of Nations*

Armed from head to foot
To hunt the dragon:
> A shaving stick
> A badger shaving brush
> A safety razor
> Ten blades
> A face cloth
> A cake of soap
> A bottle of lotion
> A comb
> A tooth brush
> A nail file

I crossed the safety coloured frontiers

As far as the eye can see
Human human misery
As far as the eye can see
At random roofs and houses
As far as the eye can see
Lingering trailing robes
Acadungemy
League of Nations

A sudden bomb explodes
Followed by long boredom
      Lingering trailing robes
      At random roofs and houses
      And the night wrestling with itself
– Goodnight, Mister Dragon!

          x

       x   x

War
Dust dust in the staircase

In the silence
The moon makes my weapons gleam:
      A shaving stick for false beards
      A badger shaving brush of pigs bristles
      A safety razor for drowned men
      Ten under cutting blades
      A face cloth in velvet
      A cake of soft soap
      A bottle mandrake lotion
      A cosmic comb
      A tooth brush in fine gold
      A nail file – phosphorescent
      So as not to forget the night
      The total night
      The night of wolves
      Where only dogs bite each other
      The cynical night
      Whispering night…

As far as the eye can see
Human human misery
As far as the eye can see
At random roofs and houses
As far as the eye can see
Lingering trailing robes
Acadungemy
League of Nations

Written c. 1943

To Put an End to the Age of Machinery the English Poets Make Smoke

To Benjamin Péret

Here are some winter flowers
Here are some summer flowers
Some trading and some lice
Some pralines and some bombs
The whole given away sold out
Lent bought thrown away

Men tremble no more
Since they have great masters
Who think for them
And foresee all

The priests and the madmen
Hooded with a sallet
Play at Pope Joan
In darkened places

The red soldiers
Are commanded by beige generals
The soldiers of blood
Are commanded by me
       Strategy of withdrawal
       Swallow your pill.

Written c. 1943

The Tree of Knowledge Uprooted, Original Sin Moves Out

To Marcel Duchamp

We have taken twenty thirty years
To live with ingenuousness
Force and ingenuity

We needed all this time
And some previous centuries
To find again the lonely tree
By the sunlit road
Of encounter and chance

Beautiful tree of Evariste Parny
Tree of entwined hearts
Behind you two beings are hidden
A priest and a detective
Armed to the teeth

Tree balloon lantern or fire-arm
The prime minister has decreed
A scene-shifting of the landscape

Same play
A roman catholic priest
An american detective
Is this really my way?

The war correspondents announce
That it is snowing in the antipodes

A priest armed with a bistoury
A detective bearded like Jesus Christ
It's wonderful!

> Flattered to have understood
> We eagerly delivered
> Our credentials
> To the Holy Father

Original sin: gone without leaving an address
'Return to sender'.

End of a Jewish tale: A lark
                A mare
                An american priest
                A roman catholic detective
                Make it into a rabbit pie
                To arms comrades!

Written 1944

Untranslatable, Statistical and Critical News Item

To Paul Nougé

        One man
        Two sizes bigger than nature
        Three hours before his death sees
        Four characters instead of
        Five appear around
        Six o'clock in the morning and it's only at
        Seven o'clock that
        Eight policeman arrived, dressed to the
        NINES

TOTAL: 45

        Statistics: Man: One
                    Hours: Sixteen
                    Characters: Nine
                    Policemen: Eight

$1 \ + \ 16 \ + \ 9 \ + \ 8 \ = 34$

Verification: Forty five minus thirty four is NINE

Critique: Easy to do
              Difficult to undo
              Impossible to re-do

N.B. You measure up to your own mistakes.

Written 1939

Vagaries

I guess, I see all manner of things...

There is a woman at the bottom of a well. Her breasts are covered with fish scales and her left arm, from which flowers a rubber hand, points to the sky with the imperturbable majesty of a mythological character.

Somewhere there is a man singing behind a fence. He represents France.

Elsewhere there is a cyclopean gardener who plants peacock's feathers in his garden and fertilises them with a glance from his single eye. The feathers take root and grow. They will be trees one day and their branches (branches of feathers) will cover themselves with little jackets and long trousers.

There is also a poor wanderer who scours the suburbs of the great towns to sell cheap goods. Alas he does not succeed, but the words that he comes to speak transform the landscape.

There is more...

I guess, I see...
And I choose from among mad men the wise.

Written c. 1944

The Sleeping Wrestler

No, no, I am not a writer like you, Sirs!
I will never dip my moon-holder into a little lakewater. Thank you.

Written September 1940

Explosive Landscape Painted from Nature

O heavy and solid cows in your wild marshes – perfumed – so sour and slow to make your bodies studded with islets ring
O heavy, o solid, o wild
O perfumed
O sour o slow
O...studded!

Written 20 November 1939

Little Prose Poem

I am the friend of all Presidents, being President myself. Between Presidents one knows what it means to talk, one understands the least hint.

We walk together to the outskirts of the town. Then we slowly climb a mountain; the highest. When at last we can embrace the whole panorama with one glance, the senior President pronounces sententiously these few words: "This, Gentlemen, is what we have never understood." A great silence follows.

Behind a bush, on the opposite slope of the mountain, a child is seated on a little pot and seems to be in pain.

No one sees him, except me. I am seized with immense compassion.

Written c. 1944

Twice upon a time
Sharing our saucers
Flying to our dreams
of hidden pleasures
We lie to one
Another's arms. We
whisper between our
legs and tell each
other's tales of red
tape and rape in the
hushed tones of mock
surprise. Every day.

Desmond Morris (1928–)

All the following poems were first published in French translation in Michel Remy, *L'Univers surréaliste de Desmond Morris* (preface by José Pierre; Paris: Editions Souffles, 1990), then in the original English in *The Surrealist World of Desmond Morris* (London: Jonathan Cape, 1991). Desmond Morris is also the author of several illustrated letter-poems and illustrated poems, an original form of combination of the written and the visual, the only one of its kind in British surrealism. Some of them are included in this edition.

The Great Wings

The great wings
of the poison penumbra
beat slowly above the heads
of the semi-intimate
as they small-talk their way home,
not a contraceptive's throw
from that breeding place of lonely houses
where pink crinkle and ivy rubber
are stowed in every love cupboard.

Written 1947

The Kettle-Headed Boys

The well placed ball tears out the breast,
pulled from the body's most illustrious folds
by unborn mutants weaned on tube-struck foam
and pits the throat with orange fins
until the shutting hinges
pinch the curving fear of stale distractions
which stain the underclothes of sterile hairs
until the cry is heard of swarming
pattern tales.

The gleaming limbs ascend the sterile hills
of calm solidity,
watched by an ear of salted yesterdays,
upon another's back,
waving to the several crowds who run apart
to show the engine's clothes
to nearby altar-pans whose single rims
reveal tomorrow's learned symmetry.

The velvet shirt unwraps,
revealing unkind telephones whose lines depart
to see the grandchild's chest of drawers,
from which a quiet sneezing sings
to the American toilet...

...while all around walk stairs
up which no hands may climb
to see the sonnet thrash from doors
unlocked to these ten sailors who,
changing their dresses,
call and tie their pockets to a shining can,
by which a laughing gate can open all our eyes.

The puckered teeth of the brain
roam around the palace grounds
searching nowhere for the uttered thoughts
which little words are needing,
and the slope is filled with the yellow desks
upon whose lobes these gentle screams
are spoken to an audience
of kettle-headed boys
whose pastimes are unheard of.

Written 5 November 1948

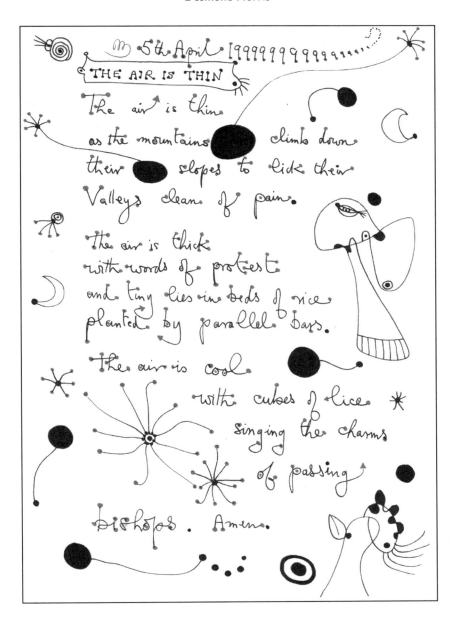

5th April 1999999999999...

THE AIR IS THIN

The air is thin
as the mountains climb down
their slopes to lick their
Valleys clean of pain.

The air is thick
with words of protest
and tiny lies in beds of rice
planted by parallel bars.

The air is cool
with cubes of ice
singing the charms
of passing
bishops. Amen.

Shoulder High

If there is a loud bang in your fingertips
never permit your reflection
to look at you from shop windows.
If you are sitting in a room with no ceiling
try and remember what time it was
when you had your first nose-bleed,
or the occasion when you climbed over
the third side of the fence of screaming reciprocals,
and heard a bell ringing in the distance.

The grass in the bedroom is damp
and it is probably better to wear
horn-rimmed spectacles
than burn your tongue.
But the heat from the mirror
that was a funeral gift
has brought on the rain.
The drops are very large
and each is falling several feet away
from its neighbours,
so that it is just possible not to get wet.
In the distance three firemen
are carrying off a plastic surgeon
shoulder high.

Written 1948

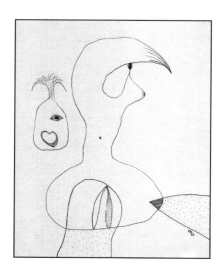

The Sideways Men

The orange flowers of the sideways men
swing from the fifty debts of the ancient bottles
that belonged to the dejected clearing
beyond the folding hills over the fence across the crimson field
where in our youth we stripped the moon.

The legs and toes of unlisted lives wave to the winged plants
of some other minute.

Below the spines of glass stems the furcoats are unlocked.

Around the sun and moon a sphere engraves its name.

The daughters of the outsides are coming in
on toads-wings feathers.

Aabbcc and the rain is dead.

Welcome to your two spheres at once.

Written 1948

Exotic Heads

Exotic heads and happy unicorns
trample the antlers of the polar saucers
in the husband's library.
The fiddle on the floor is sitting
in front of the fire
without noticing the flowers
in the chimney
and outside the air is crowded with boulders
Squares of hairs are singing in parallel
with no particular aim in view
and the suicides
on the edge of the interminable armchairs
are feeling bored.

Written c. 1949

A Small Desperation

Finding a crimson stone on the edge of the carpet,
there was nowhere to go.
There was nothing to do
except dust the weeping ornaments,
but tears are the property of the cracked glass
and should not be dried.
Their stream fertilizes the grass
which can be made of coloured metal or twisted swords.
Only now and again
can the clarity of mislaid temper
wield the blacksmith's hammer
and blow after icy blow solve this filthy honesty.
Sickness of the legs can be cured
by a wonderfully reflecting transparent rope,
but the cords hanging from the trees
are never clean enough to swing from
by one's hips.
Blood running to the head can be diverted
into graduated bottles
and the humidity may be calculated
to reveal the hideous beauty of the drop of sweat
that is about to appear.

Written July 1950

The Scented Line

Beyond the scented line,
the corrosion of my seeing limbs
grows soft with unbelievable spray
which staggers from the foliage
at your leaning feet.
The lips of my heart grow weak
at the threshold of your great vision
and my hunting bones subside,
attendant on the flight
of the white arrows' swarm.

Written February 1951

The Green Eye

Past the green eye
to the open field of incurable screens
I am driven
and wander, browsing with reluctance.
There must be an easy corner somewhere else
and a slight push in the wrong direction
would lead to a multi-coloured circle
in which black letters spell out
next year's mistakes.

Written 1952

The Face of My Brain

Your limbs are mountains
on the face of my brain.
You are walking along the tightrope
that stretches between the eyes I have for you.
Yet all I can hear is your eyelashes
burning inside my ears.

Amongst these trees a small pile
of folded sheets lies silent,
the unused sails of a sexual yacht.

There is a rug lying upon the sea
and our voyage is pursued by scissors
which cut off the buttons
of our gaping volcanoes,
as the Persians were said to do.

Written 1952

She Is...

She is a rock pool
She is the bed on which I hang my Christmas stocking
She is a furious whisper in my navel
She is a field of blue poppies
She is a sneeze in the dark
She is a coloured lantern
She is an ice-cream in the desert
She is a swarm of bees between my toes
She is a graceful yacht skimming across the sea of my brain
She is a dreaming hammock in the garden of my arms
She is a golden bottle whose label reads 'Now'
She is the ticker-tape
She is the Milky Way
She is the sphinx whose paws tread my chest
She is the purple cloud that drifts across my mouth
She is my burning snow
  my avalanche of fire
   my stick of rock
    my secret sand-dune
     my tunnel of love
      my pendulum of timeless hours.

Written 25 August 1964

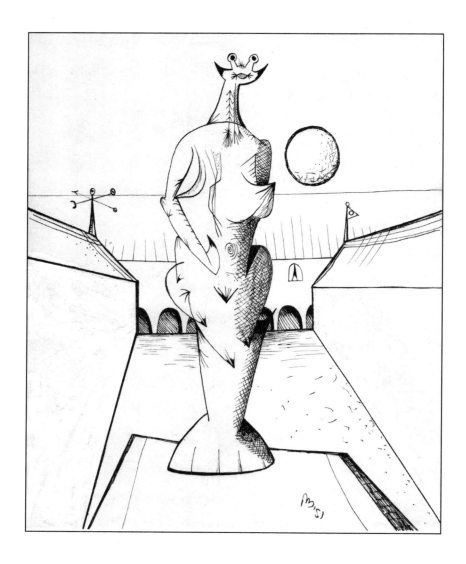

Any Body

Any body
will split the difference
and suck
the poison of a
lightning fork
spreadeagled
on the field
of love.

Written c. 1966

The Lost Art

Leaves and hair-parcels
end their days in quiet
embrace with rising fears
and soft faces watching
the frosty glass

Passing the long night
before the inner roots
begin to nose their proud
beginnings, we are deaf to
the elephant's tidy song.

Smoke slides flat in
friendly waves under the
rim of the great bowl
that used to catch our
tears before we lost the
art of angry clowning.

Written 21 April 1989

The Socket of Green

The socket of green,
close by the crowded limb,
calls to our moist palms
and dares our knotted tongue
to recall the day the clock stopped
with deep regrets that all our pains
are folded down
and stuck fast to the memory
of neglected eggs,
lying snug in the nest
of our longing.

Written 1989

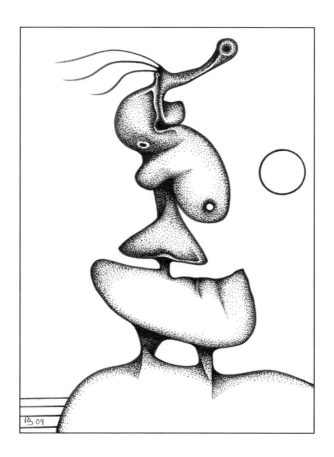

Dead faces always smile in the end
as lips retreat from the hushed
tones of spiteful praise heaped

on their silent heads as hot
necks crane their way into
the pits of the arms dealers
in their expensive black suits.
A gun is not a gun today, say the
graffiti sprayed by eyeless twins.

Grace W. Pailthorpe (1883–1971)

The Corpse

Don't go! Don't go! Don't go there!
'Tis only a dead man's bones.
You wouldn't wish to see that –
A corpse and putrefaction.
Don't go! Don't go! – whose is that corpse?
Who knows – can't tell – but none from here.
You pale. Why so? Your father's far away
In distant lands –
What can it be that you should pale at the corpse of an old man?
He is old, is he?
Then that is good, it can't be he of whom I thought.
He can't be dead.

Written 1937; published in *Surrealist Objects and Poems*, exhibition catalogue (London: The London Gallery, November 1937)

The following texts have been selected from the documents deposited after Pailthorpe's death at the Archives of the National Galleries of Scotland. They are reproduced here as written and published with the permission of the Estate of Grace W. Pailthorpe. I am grateful to Ann Simpson, Curator of the Archives, National Galleries of Scotland.

Untitled

Bloodstains blew across the sky
trailing tramps of lice and fleas
but the banjo jumped to catch
a crazy batch of bees

Untitled

I passed, quelled, 'neath the rod of iron
dumb, twisted into a shape –
not of my life's giving but of theirs
I walked, dazed and drooped with pain
to my appointed tasks.
My mind, in dismal wandering, sought another – but in vain –
half dead it sought to sense the meaning of its regimented life
and vaguely wondered to what end this mailed-fist drilling.

Time passed,
I looked around me.
All seemed wearied of their lot yet, in a stupid stupefaction,
clung to the mailed fist that held them.
Perhaps they, not I, were wise to hold the numbness of first pain
and not wake up.

Written 1937; the manuscript is annotated '"Garrick", Port Isaac, 18.1.1937'

Portrait

His hair, bamboo, was stripped of leaves
His nose a pelican's beak
His mouth a bite, his chin a bottle downside up
                              supported on a neck of twisted string
The praying mantis was his body and his limbs
His ears were vultures flapping in the gluey night
This all projected on my sight.

Written c. 1947

Untitled

Flaunting flies and teapots
I saw a train to fly
But like a mountain inkpot
It came down to a sty
Trilling like a lampost
And catching dreadful hosts
To speed upon a broomstick
It beetled up a most

Waddle to my pool you fool
And swim around and round
Flatten out your silly tum
And let me beat it like a drum
Bum, bum, bum me thumping hard
Till I have cracked the hardened shell
And now I eat you up
And then I'll spell I'll spell

Written c. 1937

Untitled

All the world's a glory
I'm dancing in the sky
tis love and life have willed
that I should fly.
Here the blue-belled wonder
with its myriad tongues
is thrumming thrilling mysteries
in wild herculic surfs.
O that one explosion could shatter me into dust
and in the welter of concussion remake my damaged crust.

Once more in dual harmony
to start life's course again;
to run and fly
and care not why
and know no mortal pain.

Written 1937; the manuscript is annotated '15.01.1937, 11.30 a.m.'

161

Untitled

No tendrilled, sap-full shoot sprang from her loin-bone
No inquisitive fingers tossed the earth-flesh aside at the exit.
Nor red flood nor marrow fruit could burst the bonded bone.
Dare the unrelenting seed beggar the womb – negate nature?
What salve will ease the venomed joint?
What is the secret thought that clamps the predestined?

Written 1949; the manuscript is annotated 'March 1949'

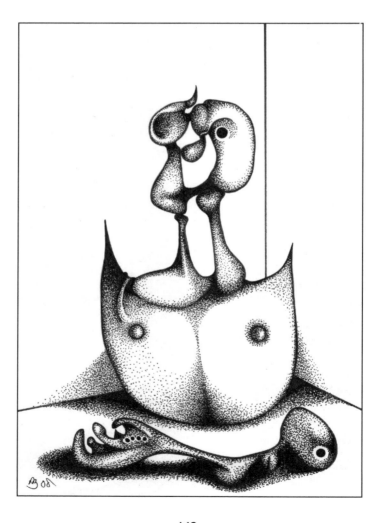

Roland Penrose (1900–84)

With the exception of 'Bulldoze Your Dead', the following texts have been taken from Roland Penrose's papers at the National Gallery of Modern Art in Edinburgh, with the aid of curator Ann Simpson. Except where otherwise noted, they were first published, with French translations, in the French scholarly journal *Pleine Marge*, 26 (Paris: Editions Peeters, December 1997).

Untitled

A sea-cow breathed from the south, blue and white
Routed in a night the cold genius
Lets drop his crystal sentinels
And cataracts removed from patient eyes
Release their tears their willow lashes comb

How could you laugh
Her mouth sealed
How could her teeth flower.
Last night the old hag died
beneath her shroud white steel
now blushing the black virgin is naked
stripped of her dress of stars
the eternal maggot stirs in her belly

Written January 1936

Ballet Mécanique
or
The Blind Man's Stick

wooden eyes the white antennae that sing
tap singing to a night of stone
while the moon presides a watery séance
between two capitals

Eastern evening
Western born.

Notice her metal dress
her face bound in links of clay
dream women chained to clouds
well armed ships passing by day
the fishes beneath their wheels are entangled in my hair.

Despised sisters tender and fair
hating themselves give birth
their unweaned child will have
their hearts in his teeth
their painted faces reversed forget the foot
caught in the revolving map of constellations
their hair sweeps the downs from Paris to New Zealand
with hands outstretched to catch them
trap shells of mountain streams
make gold her memory
Fake alchemy copper melts in ice

The little old lady still turns her crystal mirror
stroking the sea with the blind man's stick

Written January 1936

Half Born

Clothed in flowers I took her from the summer bank
a flight of pigeons lifted from her eyes
her lips became whispering shells. The beech tree's
knotted breasts murmured jealousies, its leaves
the green windows of a new world open to the eternal
open until the red hand of winter closes the door
against the faint-hearted lover
its leaves breathe
the deep waters of the sky

My love was hidden behind the branches
the badger took her by the hand leading her
barefoot through the woods
and meadows kissed her feet
with sugared lips.

The Moon has said she was to follow.
A lunatic lie, her path lay down a steep clover bed
to the stream whose white musicians hanging from the aspen
took the crown of wild flowers she had made.
All night the fauns looked down, their red eyes
saw nothing but the new born riches of a calf
and swathed in cobwebs the mother prepared
anxiously the ancient sacrifice
while the beetle messenger from wood to wood
stops wantonly on unseen flowers
this nightingale tears open the darkness and a coucou
sows his name along the field of caves.
White, the ice cold fever of her breasts I hold
only her breath the flower of her lips
speaks of the sun.

Who can make two hearts one
Devouring love the mountains for the stars
has crowned with ashes, snows and storms
their futile search
Stones fallen beneath torrent
carry for ever the scars of your feet
The gleaming crystals of the heights forget you.

My arms hold nothing
my hands clasp each other's shoulder
empty as the coucou's argument.
Earthworms, a labyrinth of insect passages
a nest of blind rats infest the unborn grass
above her form is moulded in blue
between the leaves
between the branches

the angels of the absence
A bitter shrivelled seed held prisoner in her void.

Written February 1936

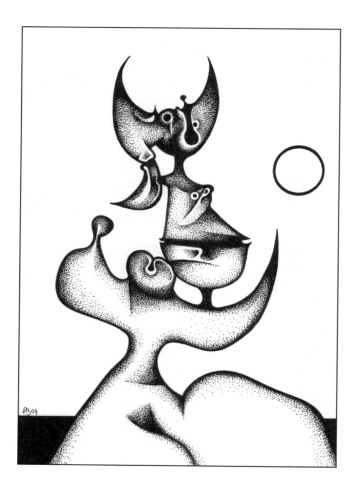

Pay Your Money

The architect travelled over the desert
No one doubted his ability to find sand
he came back with water lilies –
they went to Peking for dogs
they came back with a telescope –
he made love to the queen of Iceland
she gave birth to a louse –
he struck a match on the wall
beer flowed out –
they built a tower three thousand feet high
it is now used as a well –
they made eggshell sails perforated by the wind
dead iron with a burning heart crosses the sea faster

I wanted a sweet apple
my teeth stuck in the acid of my own tongue
I cursed the only friend who had never lied
honours and praise
I saved my last bone
the ants became bankers
I drove a forty horse power stallion
he painted miniatures with his hoofs
Tomorrow's sun has eaten his own face
the wind that blew from the south has lost its snow
of white birds for the summer
three holy priests are eating children

rewards for evil rewards
beat fresh meat out of the goat
stuff sows ears with the loot of slums
drive divide threaten burn slaughter
our preference shares yield ten per cent

looking for gold I found vermin
looking for a toad I found a star

Written in Cornwall, 1937

Portrait

The body of a porpoise its head lead
Its body a tennis court its head flies
Its body a boat its bed is a badger
Its bloody an eye its hair air
Its eye a needle its ears a bus
Its hand an encyclopaedia its land Norfolk
Its lungs a street camp its knees a saw
Its funny bone Drake's drum its nose a rose
Its ankles porcupine quills
Its nails postage stamps its cheeks a sewer
Its calves a cabaret turn its thyroid a suitor
Its arms canary cages its teeth a lurcher
Its skin smoke its tongue a walk in the dark
Its thighs windmills its sex wax
Its arse its arse its ear anything
Its brain nothing

Written c. 1939

Bulldoze Your Dead (Fragment)

1.
Follow these two men
Their music
The cross bones of their drummer-boy.

The usual Easter tune leads under the gate house
Winds through streets paved with recent war
And blocked with the bones of history.
The town smells of hunger.

2.
Coral each morning will flower from dusty windows
Gilt pictures of volcanoes repeat volcanoes
Gossip of love and destruction
Girls carry their curfew on their breasts
Streets fill and empty
Streets of soldiers marching countermarching
While avalanche the creeping wave
Drags the old castle from the hill
And corpses distil the perfume of a rotten spring.

From the twisted ribs shapeless palaces
The secret bed and crypt torn open
Runs the sore of doubt.

3.
All the seductions of the church are here
The wine of April
The serene furrows of a painted face
The green breasts of virgins
The little procession with its two bells
The lovely face blue among the branches
And the martyr riding his lion.

4.
The swaggering bullies
Their minds bellied in the mud
Have driven their teams of dark eyed peasants.
Roads like whips across the mountains
Lower the pride that millions of bare feet
Trampled and failed to tame.
A pilgrimage of buildings climbs the slopes
The sky is full of towers
Torents in paved courtyards throughout the night
The black rain of a red spring
Until the hills evaporate and the sea joins the cloud
Flashing hard bursts of steel that shine and hurt
While disease the black market of death
Sorts separates and plans its new formations.

5.
Youth has been dissolved
Youth clothed in governmental dung
Is used to stir the craters of the future
Unique piebald universal the blood
That hammers the tune of its new masters
New masters still crowned with the vultures they love.

Published in *Message from Nowhere* (London: London Gallery Editions, April 1944)

White Red Blue and Black

Eye penny sovereign world
Today you are inhabited

The gentle lawn
The scurf of bones fertilises your roots
Lawn dug into the patterns
Of a city desk
Whose banners crinkle round black windows
Royal bodice cut low on your breasts

These flags grew from destruction
Until today

Black turns to red
No night without thunder
No dawn without a flower
The twisted red of the tulip
Faithful to its destiny of flames
White lilies that play among the coal
Lilies that drop from the tails of doves
Ice to the fever
Lilies your ancient chore is in demand
Black flags clothe the surrender
Inside the fire waits
Fire of sorrow of hope

Written May 1945

Ultimatum

Lightning in reverse has signed the summer tree
The window spider's web open to estuaries
White lace iron bars
The red cup that strikes its pleasure
Through the blue limits of the veins
And the ruined girder dome through which
Mud and seaweed rain on the skin
Love which claims love
The old claiming the certain pension of death
Their children the flash the minute of the dragon fly
Greed that bursts and the frightened skeleton of thrift
Lovers whose freedom binds their hearts in angry chains
War that claims the touch of your gentle hands
The blue mirror of your head
And you who encircle in your arms the only paradise
You whose absence is the only hell

You I claim

Written July 1945

Letter Home

I

Some morning some April
We shall leave early
The harbour like a star about to rise
From the boundaries of the earth
Its stubble coloured towers guide us
Through transparent green festoons
Where the trees leap and twist
Ecstatic to the rhythm of the knife
Sweeping the flowers
With their blue fingers.

The gaiety of our company
The brightness of your dress
The blue intoxication trodden by your feet
Wraps in and out in soft pink clouds.

2

At dawn I can show you the new charter
I can show the undisputed right
To sell this bluest of seas
To meet the great liners that bring friends
Friends who have lived
Who have passed the torments
Who have spat out the squalor
And who cannot die.

The shutters of this revolting night
Are flung open
Tenebrous the labyrinth turns to crystal
The strangling thread of separation
Relaxes from the heart
And flowers grow between the monsters' eyes.

3

I left my whole heart alone
Standing by the line
The screws of travel dragged us apart
Made her smaller than a weevil's eye
Alone and cold as the fog.

Stretched my love condensed
So small so hard an atom
The universe in a tear.

Screws hooks bolts anchors
The squeaking ship its threads
Curving with the wind
Anchors itself upwards
Carries its hopes in a balloon.

And darling you who open my eyes
The wind of spring still bursts across the trees
With twenty thousand pigeons
Lizards still crack open the rocks
The sand forms golden bread
Smelling of cool walls and oil
Hunger is a friend and thirst
The freshness of dew.

And you the wonder of each morning
The warmth of your eyes
The assurance of your even breath
The naked universe in your arms
Your thighs like the rolling of a ship
The wonders from China to Amsterdam
Collected and presented by your hand
You are here
To meet the ships.

Written April 1944; previously unpublished

Orgasm

This gentle womb blue sea
White sierra and whiter sands
Prepares the birth of an army

The tinsel of flamingoes in flight
To frogs and boiling marshes
The collar of crystal foam for each grey ship
The mirrors so perfectly set
That darkness cannot squeeze into this world
Of blue rippling searchlights.

This azure sphere
Perfect poised unbreakable
Watched from the eye of the sleeping whale
Dissolves with the touch of time.

The sterile mist not life not death
Holding no desire no love
No joys no fears
This yogi virgin ice
Breaks with passion explodes
Into the light of movement.

The straights are passed
Mouth in reverse has spoken
Through the ancient perils of this dark channel
Phosphorescent tongues race towards the sky
Where last died majesty the sun.

How many have been lost
How many wrecks
Stick to the oozing passages
Lured off their courses
By the amber and red teeth
That singing line the rocks.

The movement the ocean
The new season opens
The cold unstable measure.

Eyes to your sights
Ears to your phones
Watch
The beaconing light appears behind you,
Driving commanding dispersing.
Armies to your wars
Traitors to your gibbets
Lovers to your toil.

Written April 1944; previously unpublished

Extracts from The Road is Wider than Long

These texts are extracts from the astonishing book published by Roland Penrose at
Mesens' London Gallery Editions in 1939. The book gathered poetic texts written
during his trip through the Balkans with Lee Miller together with photographs taken
by himself and Miller. The text was printed in varying fonts and colours; some words
were printed vertically, but always facing the photographs, thus creating a singular
visual exchange. The title clearly indicates the radical nomadism at work as well as
the quest for love, the desire to create endlessly.

I
They breathe with the night
in houses whose marble veins
are washed with sail cloth
whose carpets are covered with olives
whose gardens begin under the sea
they breathe with the night
enemy the SUN closes their eyes
the day of summer lasts
until the earthquake hatches
from the dream of heat
the dream of cold.

II
The road is wider than long
trees are thicker than tall
wells reach to the clouds
their blood is more solid than their bones
they have filtered it churned it kneaded it
refined it driven over it in the open fields
thrown it to the wind beaten it with flails
ground it dried it baked it in kilns

Their blood

the lion coloured forms of antiquity
stands in groups round the church
dressed in veils and embroidered coats
waiting endlessly
for a candle to be put out by the rain

they who have time have no time
it is the same today as last Friday
as the day we stole the corn
as the day she washed her hair
and it rained from the blue

have you seen the woman
age 100 asleep on the sledge
the man who lost a leg in America
and an arm at Bran
the blind man with 3 eyes
the dwarf who can play the flute with his foot

they all can sing
every jack man
and the little girl
whose breasts begin to break the plain
whose sisters lie clothed in crops
their valleys fertile
their springs sacred

Vapours escape from the rocks
writing tomorrow's news in the sky

we have forgotten yesterday
and tomorrow's news is bad news
our children need medical attention
we need a house without walls
surrounded by fire
the doors open to all who can see

our road is wider than long.

Edith Rimmington (1902–86)

The Growth at the Break

As fantasy in the claws of the poet is released by the broken arm it becomes imprisoned in the ossiferous callous wherein lice build themselves a tomb in which to escape the magic of the marvellous. Instead of, with the blood of the wound, rushing like a river to the sea – oh life orgasm – the river is dammed. The banks do not overflow and the lice choke as the arm stiffens. The wise eye sees the substitute running its poisonous imprisoned course in the cystic tomb. I see the dark sad face of the wounded man as the arm is amputated.

Published in *Free Unions Libres* (summer 1946)

The Sea-Gull

I try to catch the sea-gull with a silken cord but I find that the soft cord becomes a jagged iron chain which tears my hands. The gull flies out to sea where it sits brooding. I see it fly back to the beach to join a lazy crowd of gulls where it is fed on human flesh by tanks and guns. I am horrified by the greedy eagerness of the speckled young birds. I find I cannot escape from the chain unless I too offer my flesh to the gulls. I wait...thinking of death and living death. I decide that out of living death I may see the gull dive into the sea once more.

Published in *Free Unions Libres* (summer 1946)

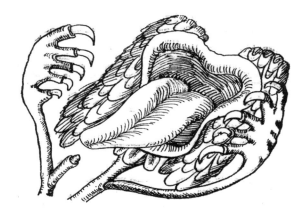

Time-Table

Death is alive in rhythm at the screech of the siren like a calm box pouring out music, projecting a life-time through endless rooms... In the dark tunnel above two musical boxes fight to be heard, heart against hub. On the ground the death chimneys vomit and always there is birth. When the music dies down life runs on wheels of search, probing for the last thought even though it is dead. After the silence of relaxation the flower buds open, exhausted, only to die from rhythm eaten roots. As death moves slowly oh the torture of waiting for a new rhythm.

Published in *Fulcrum* (July 1944)

Leucotomy

When the music of the touch hangs well then the oasis, the hair and the gasp as the tall chimneys shatteringly deliver death. The hair waves break on the shore of white picked bones, reluctantly returning to the dun of to-morrow, empty of the fury of yesterday. The starfish is dead in the empty box and the prone logs dream go-astray until the glare cuts short their sojourn and return-shocks them to the drag a chain.

Published in *Fulcrum* (July 1944)

The following texts have never previously been published, and were given by the author in manuscript form to the editor of this anthology.

My weariness returns with the same repetitive rhythm as the dog plunging into the river to bring out a stick to the shore. The one armed man with a startling look of a tailor's dummy smiled through force of habit. The children played in the grass church but the dog soon won them to the water where they threw pink flowers to toss voluptuously on the ripples. Khaki phantoms swung nameless identity chains.

The dog still brings the stick to my feet...

Written 1943

Life in the Blood

My head is full of poisoned stars, that sickness of the world, in whose bed of pain I find no rest. Where is the neither fool nor lean-to? Only the shying, hashed monstrosities hung on coat-hangers of reach-me-downs. As the hot breath of reality melts them into one with the wax figure on which they were born, they drip from the sky, their grease buds bursting to sear the ground with a congealed whiteness hiding the deep red stain – enclosing it in a tomb of wax.

Written c. 1945

A Dream

As I toss and turn on the velvet cushion memories harden the ersatz filling and as I feel the soft sand turn quick I clutch at the horse's mane.
He shies at the bright new penny and I am flung on the hard rocks.
In the many colours of my bruises I see the NEW – like the open shuttered awareness of the desert.

Written c. 1944

Untitled

I roam in the circle of silence but always the snake swallows its tail, the rope is knotted, the belt fastened and though the gate is open it closes.
In the darkness of my room I hear the sound track of misery.

Written c. 1944

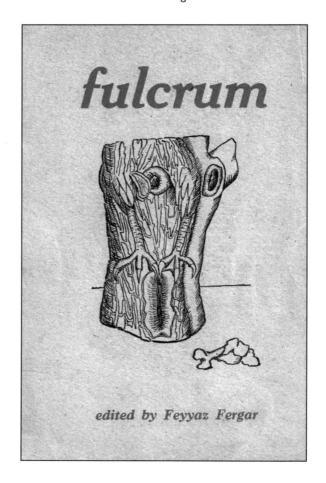

War Journey to the Country

From the hills of sleep to the plains of awake
Passed still pale apathetic tree masses,
Watching black chain-bound loads
Oil bellies…
Repressed girders
Drawn unresisting, arteries hardened,
Drifting like the smoke line, seeming to shape but ending in nothing…
Passed black houses, building death and blank.
Suddenly – DUNGHEAPS FOR GROWTH.
So speed me to the earth that I may ripen.

Written c. 1944

Colonial Irrigation

The dull blue bird coughed under the cape mackintosh as he zigzagged the moving cage singing here. We are waiting at the church. This beardless sappy whose mother carried cosmical favours should heap his excrement on his puppet father and when the cage door opens he merely hiccoughs and is sick – food for kings of predigested life.

He smells of the circus horse whose bearing-rein he deserves, that shadow of the wilderness of space.

Written 1944

Untitled

I sit perfectly still as the leaves stir and stillness becomes movement.

I am the feel of the weight of the hanging branch.

I am the birds' song and as the bird is silent movement becomes stillness revealing happiness.

Written 1945

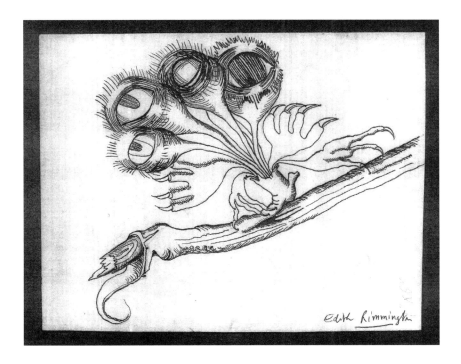

Untitled

Pale green skin fathoms fiveways – four men fright – ask yourself how?
Pale age passes – dead sink far from shame-haunts filling the hills with hard sweet swelling.
When will the eager rush of quiet silence the heavy hit of water weight down the slow slopes of tilted table tops of earth?

Written c. 1944

Aphorisms

The drying net on the harbour side is a spreading blood stain forecasting the fishes' doom.

My wasted hours shine like the full moon on the deserted road.

Noise is the sharp stone which splits the skin.

The energy of rest is to sit in the sun.

I heard thunder in the hop of a sparrow.

The worm is the lung of the earth breathing volcanic fire.

Written 1944–46

Untitled

From the first cry for the breast to the age between the pages of the yellow pension book we wake to the tearing of time.
Bank robbers pant to keep their balance before the gaol clutches them wearily.
Pop singers hear the screeching brakes of the chart and their screams fill the corners of frantic time.
The poet eases his line when the fish grows heavy as the circle on the water becomes an opening bud.
The quiet of the poisonous tongue of the snake goes with time.
As all is – all is not.

Written c. 1970

Roger Roughton (1916–41)

Animal Crackers in Your Croup

The title of the poem refers to the then very popular song 'Animal Crackers in My Soup', sung by Shirley Temple in her teens (music by T. Koehler, lyrics by I. Caesar and R. Henderson). In the song, a mother teaches the alphabet to her daughter with animal-shaped pieces of pasta which she swallows one after the other, first monkeys and rabbits, then lions and tigers, in which she sees the images of the neighbours she detests. Roughton was fascinated at the time by the Lolita-like persona of Temple.

I have told you that there is a laugh in every corner
And a pocket-book stuffed with rolls of skin
To pay off the bills of the costive
To buy a new pipe for the dog
To send a committee to bury a stone

I have told you all this
But do you know that
To-morrow the palmist will lunch on his crystal
To-morrow REVOLT will be written in human hair
To-morrow the hangman's rope will tie itself in a bow
To-morrow virginia creeper will strangle the clergy
To-morrow the witness will tickle the judge
To-morrow this page will be found in a womb
To-morrow the lovers will answer the palace
To-morrow Karl Marx will descend in a fire-balloon
To-morrow the word that you lost will ask you home
To-morrow the virgin will fall down a magnified well
To-morrow the news will be broadcast in dialect
To-morrow the beautiful girl will attend
To-morrow a cloud will follow the bankers
To-morrow a child will rechristen our London as LONDON
To-morrow a tree will grow into a hand
Yes listen
To-morrow the clocks will chime like voices
To-morrow a train will set out for the sky

National papers please reprint

Published in *Contemporary Poetry and Prose*, 6 (June 1936)

Soluble Noughts and Crosses; *or,* California Here I Come

(to E.A.)

In a small theodolite of paper
I could see the eyelash of a girl,
The most beautiful young girl of all,
Who was only dressed in cellophane,
Who was speaking from a stone
And saying this to me:
"Look out for the red and written triangle,
And enclose a penny-halfpenny stamp;
For I must go at ten to one
Ten to one it's guineas time
Ten to one will be too many
Ten to one you'll come in last.
Yes, did you hear:
My fingers hang like pictures,
And my breasts are pointing to the North?"

So I made an expedition to the Pole,
While thin birds flew off sideways with a sob;
There I heard a ringing at the door,
Where some gongs were waiting in a queue;
I played them all in turn
And presently she stepped out from a handbag,
Saying this to me:
"The happy compass is decided,
I must come at ten to one,
Ten to one's beginner's time,
Ten to one won't be enough,
Ten to one we'll get there first.
Please take this down,
Yes take this down, for purple trees will sing the answer,
For rhyming trains are meeting at a foxtrot,
For string is floating on the water,
For we are opening a parcel meant for both;
Yes please take this down, for living words are played together,
For love has grown up like a hair."

Published in *Contemporary Poetry and Prose*, 3 (July 1936)

Lady Windermere's Fan-Dance

Figures and trees in the street
Are stretching and waving their arms,
Reaching the time to repeat
The errors: result of alarms

Earlier heard in the night,
Reports they once read on a wall.
Fingers still feeling the light
Remember the hour of the fall

When gently no one had saved
With fingers in fingers of one,
Hands from the barricades waved
Or hands in the dark when they won.

Sulphurous clouds from the bank
Are killing the quick in the stream,
Bodies from gunboats that sank
Are menacing guns with a dream;

Wavering over the sun
Their arms are still greeting a king,
Holding out hands for a gun,
Impatient for shadows to spring.

Arms of the fighters of tin
Are hands of the brave of a thought
Signal the time to begin
By quietly dividing by nought.

Published in *Contemporary Poetry and Prose*, 6 (October 1936)

Tomorrow Will Be Difficult

White horses plunge hysterical through glass
And silent waters creep below the street,
While falling thunder-clouds in valleys meet
Where yellow fungus grows instead of grass.
And iron figures waiting in the pass
Stampede the shifting crowd that must retreat
Before the agony, with burning feet,
Across the barricades of broken glass.

Electric fingers clutch a waxen hand
Which crumbles slowly with a sulphur smell;
The stranger, wanting shelter, rings the bell,
Repeating prayers he does not understand.
Doors open, but the rooms are full of sand;
White bitter plants are climbing up the well,
And in the night the graves begin to swell
Until like sores they fester on the land.

And these – the loved ones with the faded rose,
The strong one not afraid of autumn light –
Together will they understand the joke
And save the Venus with the broken nose,
When carefully the old man in the night
Lets in the bailiff with the bloody cloak?

Published in *Poetry*, 49.1 (October 1936)

Building Society Blues

The vultures are being spring-cleaned,
That anonymous letter came from you-know-who;
The hawker who sold you the dangerous toy:
He meant business too.

Do you want to become an Insoluble Crime,
A lynching held in one of the parks?
You would certainly cry, though your hand were held tight
By Man Mountain Marx.

Will you cross your desires and your heart,
Finding reprieve in a suitable mass?
The Maxims they use are not to your taste,
Nor is the incense gas.

Dare you ask for a rifle and sign on the line?
Remember the pain when you fractured your wrist.
Could you bear the damp air in the grave,
Or going to bed unkissed?

Maneating plants have grown out of the bath,
The pipes are about to burst through;
Can you call for the plumber to help, with his soviet
Grammar and tickle too?

Published in *Contemporary Poetry and Prose*, 10 (Spring 1937)

Watch This Space

Under christian tree the horse and cart
Are waiting for the second vision,
And the valley river fondles indecision
Stagnant in a pastoral estate;

Lovers painted on the wall
Are gazing at imperfect faces
By the worn mosaic meeting-places
Of the weevil and the necrophil.

The singer on the private road
Has left the photographic mountain,
And aged peacocks round the fountain
Have deserted the impassive wood;

A shadow spreading from the lake
Has leapt along the careful grasses
To touch the gundog as it passes
With the paper pheasant from a book.

A voice revered across the lawn
Is blessing statues with intention
And legates celebrate ascension
In the plaster temple of the moon;

But words like his and songs like theirs
Are silenced in the silent weather,
By the cottonwool and feather,
Artificial snowfall out-of-doors;

For a message has removed the sun
And signal changed the season,
While the land expectant for a reason
Alters the anomalous design.

Published in *Contemporary Poetry and Prose*, 1 (May 1936)

Sliding Scale

Hairsprings and fingers are playing a tune
That nobody listens to, nobody needs,
Fishes with toothpicks demolish a dune
While singing the chorus at different speeds.

Hurrying kittens refer to the source
And find with their mothers it's Basic or Scotch,
Scientists claim it's the song of a horse,
Declaring that whiskey was spilt in the watch;

Error of former was due to the wells
Where truths of a sort, and another, retreat;
Singers in breadqueues are drowning the bells
Of churches and chapels by stamping their feet,

Till the young bishops ordained in the tanks
Refuse to return them their musical pipes,
Blowing instead down recorders from banks
And teaching the choir how to break up the types.

Figures on hoardings, in concerts, like bows,
When ready for leaving or lusting or birds,
Wait, inattentive to trumpeting nose,
For rising and falling and running of words;

Arrows are ardent but hardly enough
To pitch on the point counter point of the pitch,
Aimed just the same when the strings are too rough
They miss by a quaver the quivering witch.

Only the players who live in a drum,
And so can distinguish the wood from the bone,
Know the importance of rules of the thumb
And sickening terror of being alone.

Published in *Poetry*, 49.3 (December 1936)

The Foot of the Stairs

The christmas reward and the sentinel crisis,
These will be waiting for you at the foot of the stairs;
Come down, Miss O'Dicker, the young man has started
With hands and a heart and his curly live hairs;
Come down while the windows still paint you,
With cunning, the view to the east,
For over the eiderdown politics peeking
Will grow like a tumour, the girl on the beast.
Do you know of that road
So proud of its mould and wet stockings,
The purposeful safe and the wetter unlockings,
The maze that is solved with no code?
Let it be said without craft
The road was the road to perfection,
The almost, the nearly, the happy dissection
That sailed on their tide like a raft:
A raft that was made of a wood
And something more added to make it a feather;
The absolute couple can alter the weather,
The enemies know they are up to no good.
Are you awake? Did the music, the chapter,
The photo inform? Out in the air
The sparrow has swallowed the sunlight
And kindly the east wind has broken the stair.
Stairs have been mentioned before,
These are of iron and bad to the core,
Rust is their rhythm and angles their cross;
You've stolen the profit, but what of the loss?
But there is something else, Miss O'Dicker:
The prison-house governor calls here at ten;
His armament varies but he always conquers
With apple or arrow or poker or pen.
You can't see the governor's arrows
But ammonia will not take them out;
Is your linen quite clean? The skeleton kept in the cupboard
Was decently aired when no maid was about.

* * *

Have you heard enough? The jungle growl,
The desert whine, the icy ring, the city howl,
Have these played their better part?
I think they have: for that is art.
Yet the turncoats and the strip-pleas rain in crowds,
The leader gives a nickel lining to the clouds,
The fatted guns are featured on the postage stamps,
While we concentrate in concentration camps.
Clever, did you say? Life is sometimes clever:
Mountains moved by faith or faulty maps,
Railways crossing oceans at a ruler's bidding,
Rivers running constantly from kitchen taps.
No one mentioned washing up: the glasses
Only have been used; what d'you think of that?
Or could you live by bed alone? Sorry you've been troubled;
Put on your Schiaparelli apron. Mind the cat.
Now there's someone at the door; better open,
Let him see you as you are for what you're worth;
Fold your wings and brush your teeth and cut your losses,
Come down now, Miss O'Dicker, come to earth.
Down to earth? You're there already?
Then take his hand and (steady,
See, that button's loose) crisscross your heart;
The meal is served: you'd better start.

But this is hardly what I meant to say;
Now you've heard so much, will you go to-day,
Keep a secret, pack your trunks and lose the keys?
Will you do it? Please, for my sake, Miss O'Dicker, PLEASE.

Published in *Contemporary Poetry and Prose*, 11 (Autumn 1937)

Simon Watson Taylor (1923–2005)

Afterthoughts

Somewhere white clothes must fall
gently
over the hard corner of death
smiling from still mirrors
tight-lipped unbreathing

Yet I would touch with the deft twine of my mystery
the dark tower of a child's clenched fist
the burning spices of a severed head
perilously balanced over a deep reeking pit
by a thin green thread

My discarded limbs are scattered like farthings
are consumed now in the spoil and waste
of a strange city
devoured by hermits
crushed by stone-breakers
licked by parched tongues of rain
nuzzled by mongrels
for the winter's madness stretches
ineluctable and relentless as a desert's meticulous waves

Compassion the dappled cat proffers golden poison
in its wistful paws
rigid and shrinking from the thin fury
of a leaf
withered on a branch

of a raindrop
wept by a window pain

of god
dead and gangrenous

of hands
which lovers hide from daylight

of a locked door
that the wind can break down

of flags
bright as the brittle laugh of a murderer

of a bird
each shining feather a sharp malice

of love
crouched in a small unknown place

of eyes
wide in terror of their reflection in discovered water

of pools
abandoned and forgotten

of friends
wearing strange masks or faceless

of dreams
night's betrayals febrile in close minds

of childhood
ever menacing

of Time...

So with a wistful paw
I shrouded the accusing mirrors
with a snow-white cloth
that they might sleep for ever
unclouded by breath

Written February 1944; published in *Fulcrum* (July 1944)

The Sailor's Return

A newspaper full of atrocity stories
peels its diseased skin in the kitchen
the oil-lamp unfolds its wings
and revolves in prehistoric circles
seeking out with its long furry antennae
a moth's dark secret life

A day without colour
stifles the sulky window
proffers a grotesque wig
and two withered violets
to the shadows of
Three Jolly Sailors who have just entered
reeking of tar and cheap scent

One plucks a telescope from his cavernous ear
and the room is filled
with palm-trees like mailed fists
another sings a nostalgic sea-shanty
in so high a pitch
that it cannot be heard
while the third unwinds his sail-cloth cocoon
emerging as cold and dead as
Lord Nelson petrified with fear
on top of his column

and exhibits with shame and anguish
his one eye
his two hands
his one tongue
his two teeth
his one finger
and his war medals past number

Sand and shingle creep
over the tiled floor
the smell of salt water mingles
with the reek of roasting meat
the dishes are sea-wrack
and the cups shells

The lamp hovers luminous and graceful
as a painted sea-gull
and tossing on the delirious waves of
an exotic handwriting
the room sets sail

Published in *Message from Nowhere* (November 1944)

Last Reflection

Every shingle of sleeping eyes
Surges an erosion in my brain
Every tongue of hooded winds
Lights a candle in my head
Every smile of crippled streets
Weighs down my body's feather-balance
For your eyes reflect my visions
Your brain stirs foetal in my brain
Your tongue hovers a compass needle on my tongue
Your head a burning planet in my head
Your smile strokes my still-drowned lips
Your body clothes itself easily in my body

But you for ever lost
Somewhere in the day's vast maze

Published in *Dint* (August 1944)

A Shroud for Your Eyes Madam: a funeral oration

a diseased scarecrow leads the sunken febrile day
patiently by a thin red string away out of sight
among the mind's efficiently indexed bacillae
weep weep in the rivers of dazzling sky
where a sly erotic sunbeam will stroke your heliacal brow
your gnarled eyes will be shrouded by a hand of brittle thunder
lost under the anonymous rocks of the desert
yes death's waltzing typewriter will soon hammer its impossible cypher
message on your verdant brain
your blossoming brain your brain stolen by the hairy shadows
then your moss feet sinking deep beneath the iron ground

will stamp your own swollen head into the mute acephalous mire
your blindness madam will be equalled only by the horror
of your distant tapping hand's strident delirium child
your lake-ripple hand immobile as molten lava
your molten lava tongue aimless and futile as a lake-ripple
a century an impotent lust
between the ravaged thighs of time
all the nightmare's surging cavalry will erode you
bear you away spear you on their slavering crests
a mocking wreath drowned wrily in the wind's
whirling black tunnel black as absent thoughts black
and in the flickering moment of your little death remember
the lopped off fingers in the bedroom
the bleeding flowers abandoned on the staircase
the childhood fears crouched sobbing on the balcony
the folded arms tattooed round your fragile echoing heart
remember the shimmering wheels that sang in your head
your head that travelled cosmic journeys in a second's
fall
and flash
ah the matutinal woes that unfolded sedately to a faint braying of harps
sprinkling the still fragrant dust of neolithic fossils over the fat snoring carpets
the slender vases that laughed quietly in their sleeves
the vases that were brimful with coiled golden hair
with seminal fluid with corrosive tears
the vases on which naked Grecian dancers
of long long ago swayed and gyrated
m   o   u   r   n   f   u   l   l   y
ah the nocturnal problems that sidled
with sharp probing claws through your autumn brain
imprisoned between your ears that were perhaps
sealed bottle-necks never pierced by mystery's rusted corkscrew
– the conundrums forgotten for ever
always disappearing around a sudden wounded corner
with the uncertain glimpse of their white flapping tail-coats
or as dead white birds dimly seen
hovering at dusk frantic over their ancient carrion
hugging the wind's shrill circumference
geometric perspective of regrets
the death-masks of memory
and you striding backwards along the peeling avenue of your life
the floating winter leaves petrified at the touch of your hair
lie shattered on the smiling ground

who sought for love
as warm and pretty as a litter of sugar puppies
as comfortable as an onanistic rosary
as illusionary as an anadem of tumbleweeds
mock-love drawing mock-secret symbols on the pavement
dainty as a shop window full of virginal breasts and hidden tumours
– and found a demented phantom that was never love
writhing in a pit of snakes and snapping jaws
eaten away by ants and agues
rotting dumbly on an uncharted island's bald shore
encrusted with salt and blood
poor tearful ghost rocking to and fro nursing its wispy body
crying and moaning as the inhuman trees flay the sky
lacerate the effeminate clouds as relentlessly
as a needle transfixes a butterfly
cruel as the vast jungle's albino totems
yet you were clothed proudly in the fluttering ribbons of your limp moist virtue
adorned with the anile grimaces of your pensioned friends
sprinkled with the consecrated spittle of their divinely approved habits
draped with deceit's smooth seaweed skin
guarded by apathy's gaunt wan chimera
why then did you not also flaunt
the so nubile trappings of your few algebraic desires
you bright bunting flapping sodden in a thick black rain
purulent black rain falling from womb to coffin
driven howling across the grey years
so death's sleek lackeys might have stepped
a little while aside in anguish seeing
a pale flame mingled with your breath
and sperms of kisses tangled in your hair
but now the day's transparent river has frozen icy within you
the rocketing day's subtle caress stiffened into a grim statue's gesturing arm
the ignited day's miracle profaned by death's leering priests
a heart-clogging night has hardened within you
you are encompassed at last madam by heaven's verminous dwarf angels
a soft silence pressed almost intangibly against my cheek
it was only the last flicker of your burnt out day

Written 1944; published in *Free Unions Libres* (Summer 1946)

Fragments from My Real Life in Exact Proportion to Those Who Cannot Read...

A third of a hollow field-marshal's hollow baton and a sky-blue top hat are filled to the brim with little sightless butterflies: they clothe themselves easily in stockings, incredible episodes and burning grass.

***

Dressed in a smouldering glass skirt and the thousand ladybirds of a street's reared-up violence, a fragile green skeleton sat carefully upon the pure disjointed smiles of feathery angels; waiting for someone who is invariably late – the name is Richard Wagner (curious coincidence).

***

What the hell! It's raining lice and absinthe, and tomorrow's underground airport is sold lock stock and flock grazing on my hunched shoulders of sleep and torture.

***

All the toxic winds flowing out of an evil gargoyle's mouth serve to flutter a sheet of snow-white paper which is seen to hide a nipple or a door-bell.

***

A peach is eating its own stone, spitting out the stumps of its teeth, while its downy skin becomes a woman's armpit then a robot's velvet glove.

***

Alas! Alas! My lover's sex, beautiful and intricate as a hair-spring caught in a spider's web, disappears towards the horizon... which reminds me of puff-balls trailing white communion robes and twin suns lonely and eager as the shimmering testicles of the legendary wilderness.

***

Somewhere among the night's harlequin landscapes is a carving in jet-black stone of a hand vaster than a planet, raised to command silence. Under the scarlet weals of its shadow a dozen policemen dressed in the indeterminate costumes of very young children are huddled in a ring, poking at a judge's ceremonial wig with their paper truncheons; their faces are masks of fear. A dead silence hangs heavy as a grandfather clock in the still air.

***

"My dear bishop! it's as soft and fragile as trickery," said the ready-made altar-cloth, brandishing a consecrated wafer on the tip of its tongue; "do you know the story about Adam and Eve and the Glass Dog?"

Published in *Free Unions Libres* (Summer 1946)

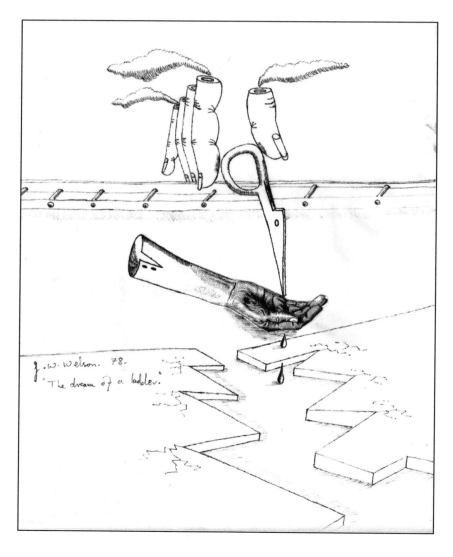

John W. Welson (1953–)

Thirst at First Hand

Waste high in kisses
The boistrous wing of pain
Needles
through he rivers of bread.
The tobacco of opening water
The breathing leather of mountains
Gloves to penetrate the sickness
of fingers soaked in ivy.

Waste high in kisses
pain
boistrous as the wing fractures
Bread penetrates the mountain
torn from the fingers of leather.
The singular gap between…
…as arms puzzle their way
through a deluge of kisses.

Written March 1978; previously unpublished

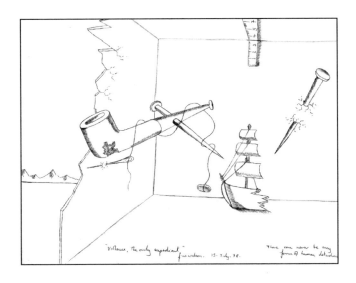

The Plimsole Line

For M.R.

These metric afternoons
without being
toothpaste beside foxes
that receive
motor cycles sideways.

These deluges
through wigwams
softened by cigarettes
diagonal fog
visited by too many regrets

Gloves
wise after the laughter,
full to the brim,
dilapidated shooting skin.

Thin gloves slash their wrists
as ice has the same lace
so legs break,
      everyone screams.

Written 1978; previously unpublished

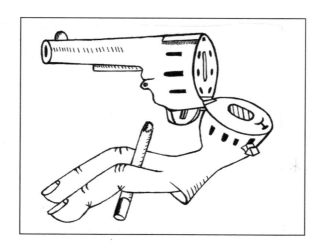

Fractured Rain

Equestrian chocolate
in avalanches of predictable yells
sprinting
between the stolen violence of stomachs
which inhabit
the blushes of footprints.

Evergreen giraffes
have the pillowcase
of an igloo
tenderly soaked in blood.

Tear up the thunder and lightning
of pepper
A beard
saturated
in the gloves of an escalator
deep in rain.

The butter of ingratitude
is a dice
balanced above the head of a typhoon in a suit.

Written 1977; previously unpublished

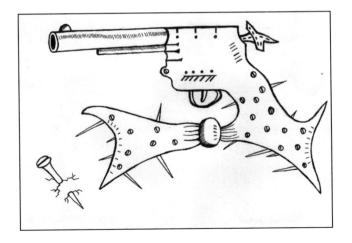

Lips of Cloud

The face below
blonde water
has no
ebbing tide
the colour of white flames

The face below
blonde fruit
has no veil
the colour of fallow candles

The face below
blonde stone
has no ice
the colour of shipwrecks

The face below
blonde crystals
has no branches
the colour of dawn

The face below
blonde skin
has a single caress
the colour of
rain left out to dry
upon the tenderness
of your lips.

Written 1980; previously unpublished

Ten and Six

I love you
on the
wall of cress

I love you
like clumsy snow
whose age
can be obtained
by looking
at the grain.

Life blood
on the wall
of cress.

The clumsy snow
of cress
in your arms
parachutes
past my lips.

To the east
there is a long plain
flanking
this agricultural land
fire
has turned all to dust

and I love you
by seeing
that fires
are illicit
and that from
your arms
cress grows
through
the age of snow.

Written 1980; previously unpublished

One Foot in Smoke

Handing down
the breath
which
is caught
in a second.

Handling breath
which
is caught
upon
your lips.

In a second
breath
is exchanged,
lips
varnished
by a kiss

In a second
a starfish
searches
in exchange
for breath
which
varnishes
your eyes
upon
my finger tips.

The colour
of blonde coal
tastes of your limbs.

Written 1980; previously unpublished

Audacious Recognition

I.

Sunlight
the shape
of a comb
the taste
of thunder
the slaughter
of drowsing
recollections
swirling
in the escape
of breath
sold cheaply

2.

Held shoulder high
these sensations
achieve wisdom,
but, all that is gambled
is the subject
of effortless muscle
nothing is devoured
as it seems to be
consumed

3.

Cool marble,
you
tasted of mud
through which
white lips
celebrate
the shadow
of love
descending
to mortal assignation

Written 1983; previously unpublished

from Spoken Flames

This city is the womb of revolution
flowers, bathed in bayonets

A smile
saturated
in the final
agonized
convulsions of a horse
fostering flies
their stomachs full
with the odious crime of christianity.

The blind gaze
at the gutter
which again tonight
will become an operating table.

The last breath
The convulsive sigh of bitterness
stinking
behind the breeze stained flag
as it smothers the blood choked drains.

Echoes of a peaceful slumber
have become a nightmare
which is shared
by the canonade
clothed in cold sweat
as you wake
at dawn

and grip your life
grasp the memory of a time
when the one in your arms
did not have the reek of death
upon her lips.
A sleeping misery.

Children
hung between the necks
of their parents

Lives purchased
by the jury
of stolen rifles.

Squandered by the sun
whose appearance
is the callous screaming of hands
who dare to touch another day.

Skin
borrowed by life;
life
that pitiful laughter
of abortion.

A single gun
sharing the lives
of two thousand
speechless eyes.

Words
spoken upon the lying nights
of belief.
Safety
born of the blindness of night
when guns move nearer the city
when women part their legs
to allow death
to dash its hopes upon another wall.

"I am the fountain of bitterness"
my wrists are slashed
by the breeze
as it drains the colour
from the flag
that throttles the tracks of tanks.
Wrists cut by the wings of aircraft.

Written c. 1981; first published in *Water Throat* (privately printed, c. 1983)

The Gift of Infancy

The mouths of children
black shields,
enacting restraint
in order that
the falling debris
of a gutted village
may not enter their stomachs.

The tongues of babies
suckle without restraint
nourished upon flames
they seize the knife
that severs all life.

Censor this echo
for its vapour
is rapidly
swallowed by their own
malignant forgery
strangled in the singularity
of infancy.

Written 1980; first published in *Water Throat* (privately printed, c. 1983)

Chronology of Surrealism in Britain

1925–1927

A few articles in scholarly periodicals mention French surrealism. In December 1925, the London Film Society shows Henry Chomette's *A Quoi rêvent les jeunes filles*, based on Man Ray's cine-portraits. René Clair's *Entr'Acte* and Man Ray's *Emak Bakia* are shown in 1926, and *transition*, an English review published in Paris and distributed in Britain, publishes translations of several poems and texts by French surrealists.

1928

First historical account of French surrealism in the *Cambridge Review*. In Cambridge's *The Venture*, Anthony Blunt declares that 'surrealism threatens to be inevitable'.

1929

Man Ray's *Etoile de Mer* is shown at the London Film Society. Edouard Roditi publishes 'The New Reality' in *The Oxford Outlook* and the film review *Close-Up* publishes an article on Buñuel's *Un Chien Andalou*.

1930

Man Ray's *Le mystère du Château de Dé* and Germaine Dulac's *La Coquille et le Clergyman* are shown by the London Film Society.

1932

This Quarter, a review edited in Paris by Edward W. Titus, asks André Breton to edit its September number. In December, Henri Fluchère, a French university professor, publishes an in-depth study of surrealism in *Scrutiny*.

1933

Exhibitions of Miró, Arp, Ernst and Dalí at the Mayor Gallery reveal surrealist painting for the first time in Britain. In October, David Gascoyne publishes 'And the Seventh Dream is the Dream of Isis' in Geoffrey Grigson's *New Verse*. In December, Charles Madge writes on the 'necessary indigenisation' of surrealism in England in *New Verse*.

1934

Two one-man shows by Salvador Dalí at the Zwemmer Gallery in May and October.

1935

In June, David Gascoyne publishes the 'First Manifesto of English Surrealism' in French in *Cahiers d'Art*, no. 10. In November, he publishes *A Short Survey of Surrealism*. Hugh Sykes Davies publishes *Petron*, the only English surrealist 'novel'.

1936

January: texts simulating madness published by David Gascoyne in *Janus*.
February: *Man's Life is This Meat*, surrealist poems by David Gascoyne, published by the Parton Press in London.
Spring: David Gascoyne translates André Breton's *What is Surrealism?* and volumes of poetry by Eluard (*Thorns of Thunder*) and Péret (*A Bunch of Carrots*, retitled *Remove Your Hat*, after censorship).
May: first number of Roger Roughton's review, *Contemporary Poetry and Prose*, open to surrealist poetry.
11 June–4 July: International Exhibition of Surrealism at the New Burlington Galleries in London (poetry reading, lectures, publication of *Le Bulletin International du Surréalisme* no. 4). Foundation of the English Surrealist Group.
October: Penrose and Gascoyne leave for Spain. *Contemporary Poetry and Prose* publishes a strident Declaration on Spain. A controversy starts with the Marxist *Left Review*.

1937

The Surrealist Group participates in the Marxist-inspired Unity of the Artists for Peace, Democracy and Cultural Development exhibition and publishes a broadsheet in defiance of the government's policy towards Spain ('We Ask Your Attention').
24 November, at midnight: opening of the *Surrealist Objects* exhibition at the London Gallery, now managed by E.L.T. Mesens.

1938

The Group is invited to exhibit in São Paulo, Amsterdam and Tokyo.
March: The Artists' International Association organises a debate on 'Realism and Surrealism' with Penrose, Trevelyan, Jennings and Read. Exhibition of the same name at the Guildhall in Gloucester.
April: first exhibition of Magritte's works at the London Gallery, followed by Delvaux's works. First issue of the *London Bulletin* (edited by Mesens, Brunius and Penrose).
1 May: the members of the Surrealist Group participate in demonstrations, wearing masks of Chamberlain made by the surrealist sculptor F.E. McWilliam.
July: Mesens and Jennings organise *The Impact of the Machine* exhibition at the London Gallery, stressing the link between the machine and the imagination.

October: the *London Bulletin* publishes Breton and Trotsky's manifesto *For an Independent Revolutionary Art*. Picasso exhibits *Guernica* and 67 preparatory drawings at the Whitechapel.

November: first one-man show of Humphrey Jennings's works at the London Gallery.

December: exhibition of Max Ernst's works at the London Gallery in aid of the Jewish refugees.

1939

January: first exhibition of Mednikoff and Pailthorpe's psychoanalytical paintings at Guggenheim Jeune Gallery. Conroy Maddox joins the group and invents écrémage.

January–February: *Living Art* exhibition at the London Gallery, organised by Mesens in protest against fascism and in aid of the refugees.

February: first exhibition of F.E. McWilliam's sculptures. Haile, Banting and Ceri Richards paint billboards in the streets in aid of the Spanish Republic.

February–March: the surrealists participate in the *Unity of Artists for Peace, Democracy and Cultural Development* exhibition in London and the provinces.

May–June: first exhibition of Roland Penrose and Ithell Colquhoun.

June: publication of Roland Penrose's poem-diary, *The Road is Wider than Long*.

1940

Brunius, Hayter and Onslow-Ford leave France and take refuge in England. In April, Mesens asks the group to redefine its allegiance to the principles of the movement at the Barcelona Restaurant in Soho.

June: *London Bulletin* triple number. Mesens organises the *Surrealism Today* exhibition at the Zwemmer Gallery and another in Oxford.

Toni del Renzio, Emmy Bridgwater and Edith Rimmington join the group.

1941

Temporary dispersion of the group. Penrose, Trevelyan and Hayter work in camouflage, Brunius and Mesens at the BBC.

1942

March: Toni del Renzio publishes *Arson*.

November: surrealist exhibition organised by Del Renzio at the International Arts Centre.

Publication of *Salvo for Russia*, a slim volume of poetry and drawings in aid of the women and children of Soviet Russia (Banting, Colquhoun and Penrose contribute).

1943

Toni del Renzio edits a surrealist section in *New Road 1943*.

October–December: violent controversy between Brunius, Mesens and Penrose on the one hand and Toni del Renzio on the other for personal and ideological reasons.

1944

Spring: Del Renzio and Ithell Colquhoun's public poetry reading at the International Arts Centre is interrupted by Mesens and others.

March: Mesens and Brunius publish *Idolatry and Confusion*.

April: Del Renzio publishes *Incendiary Innocence*, a reply to the foregoing.

Publication of *Fulcrum*, a slim volume of poetry (Mesens, Brunius, Maddox, Rimmington, Banting and S. Watson Taylor) edited by Feyyaz Fergar.

November: Mesens publishes *Message from Nowhere* and his *Third Front* poems.

1945

The Surrealist Group forms again.

September: the suicide of Sonia Araquistain, which the judge attributed to her reading of Freud, incites Toni del Renzio to launch the idea of a homage to her.

October: *Surrealist Diversity* exhibition at the Arcade Gallery. Launch of work by 'Scottie' Wilson.

1946

Simon Watson Taylor publishes *Free Unions Libres*.

December: Banting publishes the vitriolic *Blue Book of Conversation* against London's high society.

1947

Private performance of Picasso's *Desire Caught by the Tail* at the London Gallery by Penrose, Watson Taylor, Mesens, Trevelyan, Melville, Banting and others.

June: International Surrealist exhibition at the Galerie Maeght in Paris. Last appearance of the English Group as such.

1948

First exhibition of Edith Rimmington's works at the London Gallery.

1950

First exhibition of Desmond Morris's works at the London Gallery.

1951

The London Gallery closes down.

1967

After 15 years of dispersion, the Group gathers in Exeter at *The Enchanted Domain* exhibition organised by Mesens, Brunius, John Lyle and Conroy Maddox. A magazine *TRANSFORMAcTION* is published. Launch of work by Anthony Earnshaw, also Ian Breakwell, Glen Baxter, Patrick Hughes, rising stars of British surrealism.

1978

Conroy Maddox endeavours to re-launch surrealist activities in London with the broadsheet *Surrealism – The Hinge of History* and a huge exhibition, *Surrealism Unlimited*, in connection with Edouard Jaguer's Paris-based Phases Movement at the Camden Arts Centre. Launch of work by John W. Welson.

1979

The Melmoth Group is launched along with a review of the same name, together with several pamphlets and declarations. Failure to restructure activities.

Glossary of Surrealism in Britain
Key Persons and Publications

Arson (1942)

This review was Toni del Renzio's attempt to regather the members of the Surrealist Group in England, dispersed on account of the war. It included texts by André Breton, Nicolas Calas, Toni del Renzio, Robert Melville and Conroy Maddox, and illustrations by John Melville, Eileen Agar, del Renzio and Maddox. The publication brought to public notice the works of Emmy Bridgwater and Edith Rimmington. 'A spectral review glowing with its own light… testimony of a vital life lived among the ruins not only of bombed houses but of exploited people.'

Emmy Bridgwater (1906–99)

Born in Birmingham. After studying under Fleetwood Walker at Birmingham School of Art, then in Oxford and London, under Ian MacNab at the Grosvenor School of Modern Art, she had to earn a living working as a secretary. After her decisive visit to the 1936 International Surrealist Exhibition in London she met Edith Rimmington and, through Conroy Maddox and John Melville, they joined the Surrealist Group in 1940. In 1942, she contributed to *Arson* and exhibited at Jack Bilbo's Modern Art gallery. In 1946, she contributed to Simon Watson Taylor's *Free Unions Libres*. In 1947, Breton chose one of her works for the Galerie Maeght International Surrealist Exhibition. Her poems, hitherto unpublished, are haunted by the quest for origins amidst images of soaring and delving, tearing objects apart through stylistic and syntactic ruptures, the work of birth as much as of death.

Jacques B. Brunius (1906–67)

A poet, collagist, filmmaker and radio journalist, he was born in Paris and was a key proponent of English surrealism, collaborating with E.L.T. Mesens on the activities of the group after the outbreak of the war. He signed several collective texts, including *Idolatry and Confusion*, *Message from Nowhere* and *Free Unions Libres*. He published several perceptive commentaries on Lewis Carroll and edited some of the most scandalous episodes from William Beckford's *Vathek* (Paris: Stock, 1946). His filmic activities began when he was young (*Elle est Bicimidine*, 1927) and include documentaries and children's films made in Britain. His *Violon d'Ingres* (1937) is one of the first films devoted to naive art and features the Palace of Facteur Cheval as well as scenes of Yves Tanguy painting. A friend of the Brothers Prévert, he appeared in their famous film *L'Affaire est dans le sac* (1932) and in three of Jean Renoir's films. During the war, he worked for the Free French Radio at the BBC and was after the war responsible for many radio and TV programmes. He participated in the preparation of the Enchanted Domain exhibition in Exeter with Mesens, Maddox and John Lyle, but died on the eve of the opening.

Ithell Colquhoun (1906–88)
Born in Shillong (Assam). After attending Cheltenham Ladies' College she entered the Slade School where she studied under Professors Tonks and Schwabe, but also studied independently in Athens and Paris, where she met Breton in 1939. She contributed to the *Living Art in England* exhibition as an 'Independent'. Prose texts by her were published in the *London Bulletin*. In 1940, she drifted away from the group, refusing to abandon her research into the occult. In 1942 she contributed to 'Salvo for Russia'. In 1943 she married Toni del Renzio, though they were divorced a few years later. Under the influence of Matta, she painted 'psychomorphological' landscapes, whose equivalents are to be found in her texts, in search of the primordial lost unity. In 1961, she published *The Goose of Hermogenes*, an initiatory itinerary through a mythical Cornwall following successive alchemical operations. Her deep interest in Celtic lore and the mythical life of stones and animals of the Cornish heaths developed after the war (*Living Stones*, 1957) and is intrinsically linked to her experiments in automatic writing and the pursuance of her research in the occult.

Contemporary Poetry and Prose (1936–37)
A monthly, then tri-monthly, review of poetry, edited by Roger Roughton, the first to welcome English surrealist texts unreservedly. The contributors included Humphrey Jennings, David Gascoyne, Roger Roughton and friends like Kenneth Allott, Francis Scarfe (who translated pages from Lautréamont's *Maldoror*) and Ruthven Todd. It also opened its pages to poetry from Sweden, the Inuits, Russia and Japan. Politically speaking, it tried to build bridges between surrealism and communism and published the vibrant 'Declaration on Spain' against the British government's non-intervention policy. Its editions published Benjamin Péret's *Remove Your Hat* (translated by David Gascoyne and Humphrey Jennings) in 1936 and e.e. cummings' *1/20* in 1937.

Hugh Sykes Davies (1909–84)
Born in Yorkshire, a student, then a don at St John's College, Cambridge, he was a member of Experiment, an avant-garde group of graduates. A Latinist and contributor to *Criterion*, he was a committed sympathiser of the Communist Party and a member of the closed circle of the Apostles (Anthony Blunt and Guy Burgess, the two famous KGB spies, were also Apostles).

In 1935, he published *Petron*, the first surrealist 'novel', an article pleading for the 'anglicisation' of surrealism, and another article in Herbert Read's *Surrealism*, 'Surrealism at this Time and Place', published on the occasion of the 1936 International Surrealist Exhibition, at which he delivered a lecture on 'Biology and Surrealism'. In 1938, he visited Breton and Freud in Paris. Suffering from TB, he moved to Switzerland for his health. In 1940 he stood for election to the Communist Party but elections were called off on account of the declaration of war. He became a specialist in Romantic literature and published *Full Fathom Five* (1956) and *The Papers of Andrew Melmoth* (1960), the story of a scientist so deeply fascinated by rats that he decides to live with them in the sewers. Hugh Sykes Davies' legacy includes two of the most astonishing surrealist poems ever written in Britain.

Toni del Renzio (1915–2007)
Born in Czarskoe Selo into the aristocracy of Czarist Russia, he found himself in Italy with his family at the time of the Bolshevik Revolution. Engaged in Mussolini's cavalry, he was sent to Abyssinia, where he deserted from the army, disgusted by the atrocities committed there. Running away to Catalonia, he fought with the Trotskyist POUM, passed into France, met the surrealists in Paris and crossed over to England in 1940, when he joined the Surrealist Group, but broke with Mesens for ideological and personal reasons in late 1942. He married Ithell Colquhoun in 1943, only to divorce four years later. After an exchange of rather vitriolic letters in *Horizon* with Mesens, Brunius and Penrose, and their March 1944 broadsheet, *Idolatry and Confusion*, Del Renzio replied with *Incendiary Innocence* the following month. He launched the idea of a publication in homage to Sonia Araquistain, the daughter of the Spanish Republican ambassador in London, who had jumped naked from the top of her Bayswater house, the reason for this being her reading of Freud, according to the judge at the inquest. Del Renzio could not resist reacting against such decision, but there was no response, except a poem by Georges Henein and a painting by Ithell Colquhoun. In the 1950s he was a prominent art critic for several magazines.

Anthony Earnshaw (1924–2001)
Born in Ilkley (Yorkshire), he settled in London in 1933 with his family. He discovered surrealism through reading Rimbaud's poetry and struck up a friendship with George Melly. A collagist, assemblage maker, poet and great jazz and blues lover, he emblematises the anarchism at the heart of surrealism. He is the author of two dislocated and blown-up narratives together with Eric Thacker, *Musrum* (1968) and *Wintersol* (1971), and two albums of drawings (*Seven Secret Alphabets*, 1972 and *25 Poses*, 1973). He contributed to the *Enchanter's Domain* exhibition in Exeter in 1967 and to the review *TRANSFORMAcTION*. In 1981, he published *Flick Knives and Forks*,

Aphorisms, Jokes, Insults with Morals, Lies, and is the creator, together with Thacker, of the comic-book hero Wokker, a satire of modern times.

Free Unions Libres (1946)
Edited by Simon Watson Taylor in 1944 but published in 1946, it gathers texts, poems and drawings by both French and English surrealists in the hope of launching anew some kind of collective activity just after the war. Social revolution is seen as the prerequisite of a spiritual revolution inspired by dialectics. The delay in publication was caused by a police raid on the Freedom Press premises in 1944, its director, Philip Sansom, having distributed anti-militarist leaflets to soldiers at Waterloo Station. When the police found the texts for Free Unions Libres, they thought they were coded messages from anarchist groups. They seized them and arrested Sansom and a few others. A Defence Committee was immediately constituted by Herbert Read, E.M. Forster, George Barker, Stephen Spender, George Orwell, Dylan Thomas and T.S. Eliot. The story goes that the police officer who brought back the texts to Watson Taylor asked how he could join.

Fulcrum (1944)
A slim volume of poems, edited by Feyyaz Fergar, a companion of surrealism. It includes texts by J.B. Brunius, Mesens, Valentine Penrose, automatic poems by Edith Rimmington and Conroy Maddox, and work by poets from the Apocalyptic Movement such as Henry Treece and James Kirkup.

David Gascoyne (1916–2001)
Born in Harrow, he left school at 15, published the first surrealist poem written in English in *New Verse* ('And the Seventh Dream is the Dream of Isis', 1933) and an autobiographical novel (*Opening Day*, 1933). He travelled to Paris, where he wrote *A Short Survey of Surrealism* in 1935. There he met most of the Parisian surrealists, especially Eluard, Dalí and Georges Hugnet. He published the 'First Manifesto of English Surrealism' in Christian Zervos' *Cahiers d'Art* (1935), and translated André Breton's *What is Surrealism?* in the same year. After a chance meeting with Roland Penrose in Paris they both decided to 'do something in England'. In 1936, he published a volume of surrealist poems, *Man's Life is This Meat*, translated Benjamin Péret, sat on the organising committee of the International Surrealist Exhibition and exhibited objects there. In September he signed the 'Declaration on Spain' published by *Contemporary Poetry and Prose*, contributed several poems and translations, and left for Barcelona in October with Roland and Valentine Penrose and Christian Zervos to check on the preservation of works of art in troubled Spain, also speaking on the Republican radio. At that time the prey of profound existential doubt and psychological instability, he developed an existentialist, then hermetic and prophetic vision of the world, convinced

that the emancipation of the mind, in its concern for others, should avoid all kinds of ideological and religious dependence. His last surrealist appearance was with two objects at the *Surrealist Objects* exhibition at the London Gallery in November 1937.

Thomas Samuel Haile (1909–48)

Born in London, he left school at 16, worked in a shipping office and attended the Royal College of Art. First attracted to surrealism through Henry Moore's sculpture in 1934, he developed a strong interest in pottery and ceramics, taught at several colleges and art schools and joined the Surrealist Group in 1937, showing paintings in the surrealist room at the A.I.A. mammoth exhibition in April, and objects at the Surrealist Objects exhibition at the London Gallery in November. A most committed surrealist painter and potter, he turned pottery and canvas into dissecting tables, breaking down the barrier between the two arts and operating upon figures and objects with a deeply wry, and somehow despondent, humour. A vehement anti-colonialist and pacifist, he left England in 1939 just before the outbreak of the war for the United States, where he lectured at Alfred University in New York and Ann Arbor until 1944. Back in England, he resumed pottery but died in a car accident in Poole (Dorset) in 1948. He left an unpublished notebook in which he proves to be a very perceptive theoretician of surrealism.

Idolatry and Confusion (1944)

A violent pamphlet published in 1944 by the London Gallery Editions and written by Mesens and Brunius against Del Renzio, the third step of a quarrel which started with accusations of stealing texts from their authors and an exhibition organised by Del Renzio and Ithell Colquhoun at the International Arts Centre in 1942 and developed with vitriolic letters in *Horizon* and *Tribune*. The ostensible subject of the pamphlet was a scathing criticism of Louis Aragon and French Resistance literature, but the real target was Del Renzio, who 'tries to imitate Breton'.

Incendiary Innocence (1944)

Dated 4 April 1944 ('Lautréamont's Day'), this pamphlet by Toni del Renzio redefines the surrealist standpoint and reiterates his faithfulness to André Breton's principles by summing up surrealism's view of Freud, the 'supreme point' notion, the importance of Hegelian dialectics and of the alchemical and hermetic tradition. Criticising Eluard's recent poetry (just translated into English by Mesens and Penrose), he advocates an exploration of myths, especially the myth of the androgyne, and extols monogamy.

Humphrey Jennings (1907–50)
Born in Walberswick (Suffolk), he studied at Cambridge where, as a student in drama, he designed theatrical settings and costumes for various productions. From 1931 onwards, he regularly went to Paris, establishing links between French artists and the Cambridge avant-garde of the review *Experiment*. In 1934 he started to work for John Grierson's GPO Film Unit, made several short features (for publicity and animation), sat on the organising committee of the International Surrealist Exhibition in London in 1936, exhibited there, translated Benjamin Péret with David Gascoyne and wrote short texts, which he called 'reports', for *Contemporary Poetry and Prose*. He exhibited with the surrealist group in Paris, Amsterdam and London, held his first one-man show at the London Gallery in 1938 and contributed to the *Living Art in England* exhibition in 1939, also acting as assistant director of the *London Bulletin*. He was excluded from the group for having made documentary films extolling the war effort and for having accepted the OBE. For thirteen years, he worked on *Pandaemonium*, a huge volume of texts which he compiled from the writings of factory workers, scientists, journalists, inventors, dukes and actresses, all dealing with how the human imagination produced and experienced the impact of machines from the Industrial Revolution onwards (edited in 1985 by Charles Madge and Mary-Lou Jennings). He died on the island of Poros in Greece.

Sheila Legge (1909?–48?)
A friend of David Gascoyne and Dylan Thomas, she first appeared at the International Surrealist Exhibition in London in June 1936, not only by exhibiting several objects but also by appearing in Trafalgar Square wearing a long satin dress, a bunch of roses on her face, an artificial leg in one hand and a pork chop in the other. She published one text in *Contemporary Poetry and Prose*, exhibited an object at the *Surrealist Objects* exhibition at the London Gallery in November 1937 and, phantom-like, disappeared.

***The London Bulletin* (1938–40)**
Edited by E.L.T. Mesens, successively assisted by Humphrey Jennings, George Reavey and Roland Penrose (who was the main source of finance), and published by the London Gallery, its initial goal was to publish texts related to the gallery's exhibitions. It did publish the catalogues of the first solo exhibitions of F.E. McWilliam, Ithell Colquhoun, Roland Penrose and Humphrey Jennings and among its contributors counted Magritte, Read, Scutenaire, Marcel Mariën, Conroy Maddox and Paul Nash. In October 1938, it published in French the 'Declaration for an Independent Revolutionary Art' written by Breton and Trotsky in Mexico, in January 1939 Grace Pailthorpe's 'The Scientific Aspects of Surrealism', and in June 1940 Conroy Maddox's seminal

text on the object. The journal had no doctrinal or theoretical position as such but a strong determination to build an artists' united front against fascism.

Len Lye (1901–80)
Born in Christchurch (New Zealand), where he attended the local College of Art, he crossed to Australia where he did some labouring work in the outback and worked his passage to London as a stoker on a liner in 1926. He settled there, living on a barge in Hammersmith, and constructing mobiles in wood and metal. He met Robert Graves, Laura Riding and Ben Nicholson and became a member of the constructivist group, the Seven and Five Society. In 1928 he made a remarkable abstract animation film, *Tusalava*, worked with Eisenstein and Richter, and published *No Trouble* in 1930, a series of prose-poetry letters. In 1935, he made the first ever film without a camera, *Colour Box*, by scratching and colouring the film itself, and started to work with Humphrey Jennings on films for John Grierson's GPO Film Unit. In 1936, he took part in the International Surrealist Exhibition in London and joined the group, taking part in most of its activities, also contributing to the *London Bulletin*. In 1944 he was appointed director of the *March of Time* news documentary film series and emigrated to the United States in 1951, returning to experimental film-making and taking up kinetic sculpture in 1958.

Conroy Maddox (1912–2005)
Born in Ledbury, he studied in Birmingham, discovering surrealism by chance when thumbing through books such as R.H. Wilenski's on modern art at Birmingham Library. He met John and Robert Melville with whom he signed a letter to Roland Penrose in 1936 refusing to take part in the International Surrealist Exhibition, the choice of the English works appearing too lax to them. In 1937, he went to Paris where he befriended Matta, Man Ray, Gordon Onslow Ford and Georges Hugnet. On his return he joined the English group. He published a seminal article on the object in the *London Bulletin* in June 1940, contributed to Del Renzio's *Arson* in 1942 and published a series of anti-religious and iconoclastic texts and aphorisms entitled 'The Exhibitionist's Overcoat' in various magazines. He contributed to *New Road 1943*, *Message from Nowhere* and *Free Unions Libres*. Before the war, he invented 'écrémage', a semi-automatic technique, and from 1944 on found himself the 'leader' of a group of artists in Birmingham, one of whom was Desmond Morris. In 1967, he co-organised the *Enchanter's Domain* exhibition in Exeter with Mesens, Brunius and Lyle, and contributed to most issues of Lyle's *TRANSFORMAcTION*. From the seventies on, he gathered around him in London a nucleus of surrealist artists with whom he founded the group and short-lived magazine both called *Melmoth* (1979). In 1978, he mounted the *Surrealism Unlimited* exhibition at the Camden Arts Centre,

to which the French Phases movement was invited. Conroy Maddox may be considered one of the most thoroughgoing British surrealists.

Reuben Mednikoff (1906–76)

Born in London, he entered St Martins School of Art at the age of 15 and worked in advertising, befriending David Gascoyne, Dylan Thomas, Julian Symons and Pamela Hansford Johnson. At a friend's party he met the 52-year-old psychoanalyst Grace Pailthorpe, with whom he began a lifelong relationship, introducing her to art while she introduced him to psychoanalysis. They spent time in Cornwall where they explored each other's subconscious in a strictly reciprocal and systematic collaboration. Their work featured in surrealist exhibitions from the 1936 London International Surrealist Exhibition – where André Breton admired their work – up to the outbreak of war. Their first show was organised by the Guggenheim Jeune Gallery in London in 1939. In 1940, they were excluded from the group for refusing to exhibit with the group only. In the same year they emigrated to the United States and then to Vancouver, Canada, where they exhibited, lectured and founded the Association for the Scientific Treatment of Delinquency. In 1948 Mednikoff was legally adopted by Grace Pailthorpe under the name of Richard Pailthorpe. In 1955 Mednikoff opened an antique shop in Battle. He never recovered from the shock of Pailthorpe's death in 1971 and died himself in 1976.

George Melly (1926–2007)

A poet, essayist, blues and jazz singer, born in Liverpool, he joined the Navy at the age of 18 and served for three and a half years. Attracted by anarchism, he discovered surrealism through reading David Gascoyne's *Short Survey of Surrealism* among other publications, contacted Mesens, the Director of the London Gallery, and worked as the secretary of the Gallery. He toured England as a blues singer. He then worked for the *Daily Mail*, creating a daily comic strip, *Flook*, featuring a caustic and subversive surrealist-minded character. Having become TV, music and cinema reviewer for the *Observer*, he devoted himself increasingly to blues and jazz singing from 1971 onwards. He wrote several chronicles of the sixties and the pop generation, but his book on Scottie Wilson, a surrealist 'outsider' discovered by Mesens and Penrose in 1945, reveals his profound attachment to the surrealist spirit.

Edouard Léon Théodore Mesens (1903–71)

Born in Brussels, 'without god, without master, king or rights' as he said, he was a pivotal figure in the history of Belgian surrealism, publishing most of its magazines, managing a gallery and maintaining long-lasting links with the French group, until 1937 when he settled in London and ran the London Gallery with the financial help of Roland Penrose. He edited the 20 issues of *The London Bulletin* from 1938 till 1940, organised all the group's shows as well as solo exhibitions of British surrealists, and made repeated attempts to re-form the group. With J.B. Brunius he co-authored the pamphlet *Idolatry and Confusion* attacking Del Renzio, and published *Message from Nowhere* in 1944. His last attempts to gather the group were the *Surrealist Diversity* exhibition at the Arcade Gallery in 1945 and the *Enchanter's Domain* exhibition at Exeter in 1967, co-organised with Brunius, John Lyle and Conroy Maddox. As a collagist he loved to combine typographic signs and banal images into visual puns. He was one of the most fervent proponents of surrealism and a staunch defender of modern art.

Message from Nowhere (November 1944)
Edited by E.L.T. Mesens and published by London Gallery Editions, this attempt to rekindle the surrealist spirit opens with a bilingual editorial by André Breton – an extract from his speech to the Yale students in 1944 – and includes poems (in French as well as in English) by Jarry, Mesens, Penrose, S. Watson Taylor and Patrick Waldberg, with notes by Banting, Maddox and others and drawings by Banting, Edith Rimmington and Picasso.

Desmond Morris (1928–)
Born in Purton (Wiltshire), he was the child of an author of children's stories and the grandson of a naturalist. Attracted by nature and sciences as well as drawing, he was encouraged by the art critic Mervyn Levy to develop his abilities in the field of art. In January 1948, his first exhibition in Swindon was the butt of scathing reviews in the local press. He then started zoology studies but in 1949 he joined the group of surrealist artists who gathered around Conroy Maddox in Birmingham, exhibiting at the London Gallery in a joint show with Miró in 1949. He made two films, *The Flower of Time* and *The Butterfly and the Pin*. In 1956, as the director of the Film Unit of the Zoological Society of London, he became interested in chimpanzees' ability to draw and paint, mounting an exhibition of their works, which, needless to say, created uproar. In 1962 he wrote *The Biology of Art* and in 1964 he entertained Miró at the London Zoo. He served for a time as Director of the Institute of Contemporary Art. In 1967 the phenomenal worldwide success of *The Naked Ape* allowed him to devote himself entirely to the ethological study of animal and human mores and to the painting of wriggling biomorphs and amoeba-like forms, displaying his fascination with the origins of life, both physical and mental. In 1983 he wrote *Inrock*, a fantasy taking place inside rocks. He lives in Oxford.

New Road 1943
A literary review founded by Alex Comfort and John Bayliss, printed by the Grey Walls Press in Billericay (Essex). In November 1943, a 50-page section

of the review was devoted to surrealism under the editorship of Toni del Renzio. It opened with an article on monogamy, followed by texts by Ithell Colquhoun, Robert Melville (on Chirico), André Breton, Kurt Seligman (on sadism), Nicolas Calas (on Tanguy) and Max Ernst (on himself), aphorisms by Conroy Maddox and poems by Georges Henein, Valentine Penrose, Toni del Renzio, Aimé Césaire and Charles-Henri Ford. This publication, accused by Mesens of having used texts without permission, was the starting point of a long and violent exchange between Del Renzio and Mesens.

Grace W. Pailthorpe (1883–1971)
Born in Sutton (Surrey), she first studied medicine, working as a doctor during the First World War and then specialising in criminal psychology. In 1931 she founded the Association for the Scientific Treatment of Criminals and wrote two books on the subject and on imprisonment. In 1935, at a friend's party, she met the 29-year-old artist Reuben Mednikoff with whom she started a lifelong collaboration resulting in the prolific creation of images and texts. Alongside Mednikoff, she was chosen to show at the London International Surrealist exhibition in 1936, where Breton praised her work. A member of the group, she exhibited with them in England and abroad until 1940. After their first joint exhibition at the Guggenheim Jeune Gallery in London in 1939 and a controversial article, 'The Scientific Aspects of Surrealism', in the *London Bulletin* that same year, Pailthorpe and Mednikoff left for the USA and then Canada (British Columbia), where they both lectured, organised exhibitions and founded the Association for the Scientific Treatment of Delinquency. Back in England after the war, she opened a private practice in Wimpole Street, London, then settled in Bexhill (Sussex) where she died, five years before Mednikoff, whom she had adopted as her son in 1948.

Roland Penrose (1900–84)
Born in London, he studied architecture in Cambridge but, wanting to escape from his complacent Quaker family environment, left England at the age of 22 for Paris and, until 1935, the south of France, where he met Valentine Boué, who became his wife. In Paris, he attended the surrealist group's meetings, be-friending Eluard, Ernst, Miró and Man Ray. In 1935, through Eluard, he met David Gascoyne in Paris, and they both decided to 'export' surrealism into England. The following year, the organising committee of the International Surrealist Exhibition was established and Penrose showed paintings and objects there. In November that year, he signed the 'Declaration on Spain' published by the Surrealist Group in *Contemporary Poetry and Prose* and went to Spain with Valentine, David Gascoyne and Christian Zervos, the editor of *Cahiers d'Art*, to check on the rumours of the destruction of art works by the Republicans. In 1937, he helped Mesens to become director of the London Gallery and to launch the *London Bulletin*. He then took part in all surrealist

activities and exhibitions in England and abroad. In 1938, the year he bought Eluard's entire collection of paintings, he fell in love with Lee Miller, once Man Ray's assistant and a celebrated photographer, whom he met at a Parisian 'soirée', and left with her for the Balkans in 1939. From that trip he brought back the astonishing *The Road is Wider than Long*, a book-poem made up of texts with varying typography and photographs taken by him and Miller, a celebration of unexpected encounters and of the freedom of love. During the war he worked in camouflage, signed *Idolatry and Confusion* with Mesens and Brunius, translated Eluard's *Poésie et Vérité* and collaborated on *Salvo for Russia* (1942), *Message from Nowhere* (1944) and *Free Unions Libres* (1946). In 1947, he produced the performance of Picasso's *Desire Caught by the Tail* at the London Gallery. He founded the Institute of Contemporary Art in 1950 and helped to organise the *Enchanter's Domain* exhibition in Exeter in 1967 with Mesens, Lyle and Maddox. He is famous for his postcard collages in which the juxtaposition and reordering of picture postcards reveals unsuspected rhythms and forms. Breton called him a 'surrealist in friendship'.

Edith Rimmington (1902–86)

Born in Leicester, she first appeared with the surrealist group at the *Surrealist Objects and Poems* exhibition in November 1937 and participated in all its various manifestations. She contributed drawings and automatic texts to the *London Bulletin*, *Arson* (1942), *Fulcrum* (1944), *Message from Nowhere* (1944) and *Free Unions Libres* (1946). Along with Ithell Colquhoun and to a certain extent Emmy Bridgwater, she was one of few British surrealists to explore automatism in writing. Her work was chosen by André Breton to feature at the Galerie Maeght International Surrealist Exhibition in 1947. She settled in Bexhill-on-Sea where she devoted herself to photographing beaches, pebbles, boats aground and driftwood.

Roger Roughton (1916–41)

A member of the informal group of poets who gravitated around David Archer's Parton Press – with David Gascoyne, Gavin Ewart and Dylan Thomas among others – he adhered to the Communist Party in the early thirties, which explains his many desperate attempts to link the communist ideal and the surrealist approach. In May 1936, he launched *Contemporary Poetry and Prose*, which printed poems by French and English surrealists and fellow-travellers of surrealism, such as Francis Scarfe and Kenneth Allott, as well as ritual texts from different ethnic groups. In November 1936, he published the group's 'Declaration on Spain'. Profoundly disappointed by his failure to create a united front of Trotskyists, communists and surrealists, and escaping the draft on the eve of the Second World War, he left for Dublin, his native city, where he committed suicide in 1941.

Salvo for Russia (1942)

A slim volume of four poems by Cecily Mackworth, James Law Forsyth, J.F. Hendry and Nancy Cunard, published to aid the Support Funds for Women and Children of Soviet Russia, accompanied with engravings by many artists, including John Banting, Ithell Colquhoun, Roland Penrose, Mary Wykeham and John Buckland-Wright, the latter two ephemeral members of the surrealist group. An example of the political involvement of English surrealism.

Simon Watson Taylor (1923–2005)

He joined the Surrealist Group in 1940 at one of its meetings at the Barcelona Restaurant and contributed iconoclastic texts and poems to *Fulcrum* (1944), *Dint* (1944) and *Message from Nowhere* (1944). In 1944 he started to gather material for *Free Unions Libres*, translating texts by Benjamin Péret, Alfred Jarry, Mesens and de Sade and writing two long poems. That year, while raiding the Freedom Press, whose director, Philip Sansom, had been arrested for distributing anti-militarist leaflets at Waterloo Station to soldiers on their way to the front, the police found Watson Taylor's address, went to see him and hit upon proofs of *Free Unions Libres*, which they thought were anarchist coded messages. These were soon given back but the delay explains why the book was published only in 1946. In 1945, he served as secretary to the London Gallery. In constant touch with the French surrealists, he did his best to preserve the unity of the English group, but to no real avail. He became a Pataphysician and ended his life travelling around the world.

John W. Welson (1953–)

One of the most intransigent and faithful surrealists of the third generation. He helped Conroy Maddox to re-launch activities in London from 1973 onwards, founding the Melmoth Group in 1980 with Roger Cardinal, Michael Richardson and others. In 1978 he took part in the Camden Arts Centre *Surrealism Unlimited* exhibition, co-edited *The Hinge of History* as a supplement to *Freedom* (an anarchist bi-monthly), and wrote a series of theoretical proposals on surrealism. In the same year, he organised the *Terrain of the Dream* exhibition in Wales, which gathered a vast number of surrealist works from all over the world – some of the works being physically attacked during the exhibition. In 1982 he published a volume of poems, *Water Throat*. In 1985, he resigned from his job as a civil servant and settled in Fishguard (Wales), where he produces abundant oils, gouaches and drawings, veritable 'cosmic muscles and entrails', which introduce a new 'visceral-gestural element in surrealist painting', according to Edouard Jaguer, the 'leader' of the Phases movement in France.

Select Bibliography

British surrealist publications

Arson: An Ardent Review. Part One of a Surrealist Manifesto, ed. Toni del Renzio (March 1942).

Contemporary Poetry and Prose, ed. Roger Roughton, 1.1 (May 1936)–1.8 (December 1936) and 2.9 (Spring 1937)–2.10 (Autumn 1937).

Free Unions Libres, ed. Simon Watson Taylor (London: Freedom Press, summer 1946).

Fulcrum, ed. Feyyaz Fergar (July 1944).

Idolatry and Confusion, ed. E.L.T. Mesens and J.B. Brunius (London: London Gallery Editions, March 1944).

Incendiary Innocence, an Arson pamphlet, ed. Toni del Renzio (April 1944).

London Bulletin, ed. E.L.T. Mesens, 1 (April 1938)–18-20 (June 1940).

London Gallery Express, an occasional news-sheet (London: London Gallery, March–April 1947).

London Gallery News, an occasional paper (London: London Gallery Editions, December 1946).

Message from Nowhere, ed. E.L.T. Mesens (London: London Gallery Editions, November 1944).

New Road 1943, ed. Alex Comfort and John Bayliss (Billericay: Grey Walls Press).

Salvo for Russia, an edition of etchings and engravings, in aid of the Comfort Fund for Women and Children in Soviet Russia, ed. Nancy Cunard and John Banting (London, 1942).

TRANSFORMAcTION, ed. John Lyle (Sidmouth, Devon), 1 (1964)–10 (1980).

Major surrealist exhibitions and catalogues

1971 *Britain's Contribution to Surrealism of the 30s and 40s*, London, Hamet Gallery (3–27 November).

1978 *Dada and Surrealism Reviewed*, London, Hayward Gallery (11 January–27 March). Catalogue edited by Dawn Ades, intr. David Sylvester. Texts by Dawn Ades and Elizabeth Cowling.

1985 *A Salute to British Surrealism 1930–1950*, Colchester, The Minories (6 April–5 May). Texts by Michel Remy and Mel Gooding.

1986 *La Planète Affolée, Surréalisme – Dispersion et Influence 1938–1947*, Marseilles, La vieille Charité (12 April–30 June). Texts by José Perre, Edouard Jaguer, Michel Fauré, José Vovelle, Sarah Wilson, Martica Sawin and others.

British Surrealism, Fifty Years On, London, The Mayor Gallery (March–April). The exhibition then went on to Middlesbrough Art Gallery (24 May–14 June). Text by Michel Remy.

Surrealism in England, 1936 and After, Canterbury, Canterbury College of Art (19–31 May). Texts by Duncan Scott, Toni del Renzio and Michel Remy. The exhibition then

228

travelled to the National Museum of Wales, Cardiff (August–September) and to the Laing Gallery, Newcastle (October–November).

Contrariwise, Swansea, Glynn Vivian Art Gallery (20 September–15 November). Texts by Ian Walker (curator), J.H. Matthews, George Melly. The exhibition then went on to the Victoria Art Gallery, Bath (November–January), the Polytechnic Gallery, Newcastle (January–February) and the Mostyn Art Gallery, Llandudno (February–April 1987).

1988 *I Surrealisti*, Milan, Palazzo Reale, org. Arturo Schwarz (16 May–13 September). Catalogue by Edizione Mazzotta, Milan. Texts by José Vovelle, Martica Sawin, Michel Remy and others.

1991 *The Birmingham Seven*, London, John Bonham and Murray Feely Fine Art (12 June–13 July). Texts by Michel Remy and Murray Feely.

1994 *British Surrealism 1935–1994*, London, England and Co. (5–27 May). No catalogue.

2000–2001 *Surrealism in Birmingham 1935–1954*, Birmingham, Birmingham Museums and Art Gallery (9 December 2000–11 March 2001). Texts by Silvano Levy, Tessa Sidey, Lisa Rüll, Phoebe Tulip and Michel Remy.

2009 *British Surrealism in Context, A Collector's Eye – The Jeffrey Sherwin Collection*, Leeds, Leeds Museums and Galleries (10 July–1 November). Texts by Michel Remy, Silvano Levy, Jeffrey Sherwin and Jon Wood.

2010–11 *Another World: Dalí, Magritte, Miró and the Surrealists*, Edinburgh, The National Galleries of Scotland (10 July 2010–9 January 2011). Text by Patrick Elliott.

Works on surrealism in general

Alquié, Ferdinand, *Philosophie du Surréalisme* (Paris: Flammarion, 1955), trans. *The Philosophy of Surrealism* (Ann Arbor: University of Michigan Press, 1969).

Breton, André, *Le Surréalisme et la Peinture* (Paris: Gallimard, 1965), trans. by Simon Watson Taylor, *Surrealism and Painting* (New York: Harper and Row, 1972).

Breton, André, *What is Surrealism?* (New York: Haskell House, 1974).

Cardinal, Roger and Short, R.S., *Surrealism, Permanent Revolution* (London: Studio Vista; New York: Dutton, 1970).

Chadwick, Whitney, *Myth in Surrealist Painting 1924 to 1939* (Ann Arbor: University of Michigan Press, 1980).

– *Women Artists and the Surrealist Movement* (London: Thames and Hudson, 1985).

Guggenheim, Peggy, *Art of This Century 1910–1942*, preface by André Breton (New York, 1942).

Jean, Marcel (and Arpad Mezei), *Histoire de la peinture surréaliste* (Paris: Seuil, 1959), trans. by Simon Watson Taylor, *History of Surrealist Painting* (London: Weidenfeld and Nicolson, 1962).

Levy, Silvano (ed.), *Surrealism: Surrealist Visuality* (Keele: Keele University Press, 1996).

Lippard, Lucy, *Surrealists on Art* (Englewood Cliffs: Prentice Hall, 1970).

Matthews, J.H., *Surrealism and the Novel* (Ann Arbor: University of Michigan Press, 1966).

– *Surrealism and Film* (Ann Arbor: University of Michigan Press, 1971).

– *Towards the Poetics of Surrealism* (Syracuse: Syracuse University Press, 1976).

– *The Imagery of Surrealism* (Syracuse: Syracuse University Press, 1977).

Pierre, José, *L'Univers Surréaliste* (Paris: Somogy, 1983).

Read, Herbert (ed.), *Surrealism* (London: Faber and Faber, 1936). Essays by Herbert Read, André Breton, Paul Eluard, Hugh Sykes Davies and Georges Hugnet.

Rosemont, Franklin, *What is Surrealism?* (New York: Monad Press/Pathfinder Press, 1978).

Works on surrealism in Britain

Books

Germain, Edward B., 'Surrealist Poetry in English 1929–1947', originally a PhD thesis, University of Michigan, Ann Arbor (1969); published in shortened form as the introduction to *English and American Surrealist Poetry*, ed. E.B. Germain (Harmondsworth: Penguin Books, 1978).

Jaguer, Edouard, and Remy, Michel, *La Peinture surréaliste en Angleterre 1930–1960: Les Enfants d'Alice*, catalogue of an exhibition at the Galérie 1900–2000, Paris, 1982.

Ray, Paul C., *The Surrealist Movement in England* (New York: Cornell University Press, 1971).

Remy, Michel, *Surrealism in Britain* (London: Ashgate/Lund Humphries, 1999, 2001).

Articles

Blunt, Anthony, 'Superrealism', *Spectator*, 156 (18 June 1936), 1125–27.

Byrne, Barry, 'Surrealism passes', *Commonweal*, 26 (2 July 1936), 262–63.

Connolly, Cyril, 'It's Got Here at Last', *New Statesman*, 10, 251 (14 December 1935), 946.

Matthews, J.H., 'Surrealism and England', *Comparative Literature Studies*, 1.1 (1964), 55–72.

Plomer, William, 'Surrealism Today', *New Statesman*, 19 (29 June 1940), 794.

Remy, Michel, 'Le Surréalisme et la politique en Angleterre', SAES Symposium in Nantes, Paris, Didier (Coll. Etudes Anglaises), 185–96.

– 'La vraie nature du surréalisme: le surréalisme en Angleterre', SAES Symposium in St Etienne, Paris, Didier (Coll. Etudes Anglaises), 67 (1975), 107–16.

– '1936, l'année de tous les dangers', *Mélusine* (Cahiers du Centre de Recherches sur le Surréalisme), 8 (Winter 1986), 125–42.

– 'The Visual Poetics of British Surrealism', in *Surrealism*, ed. Silvano Levy (Keele: Keele University Press, 1995).

Short, Robert S., 'Le Surréalisme en Grande-Bretagne', *Bulletin du Centre National de la Recherche Scientifique*, Paris (9 October 1978).

Wilson, Sarah, 'En Angleterre', in *La Planète affolée*, catalogue of an exhibition in Marseilles (April–June 1986) (Paris: Flammarion, 1986).

Works by and on individual British surrealists

In the following sections, primary creative works precede critical studies and articles.

Bridgwater, Emmy

'The Birds', *Free Unions Libres* (Summer 1946), 33.

Deepwell, Katy (and D. Sugg), 'Emmy Bridgwater', *Women's Art Magazine*, 37 (November–December 1990), 16–19.

Hall, Charles, 'Review: Emmy Bridgwater at Blond Fine Art', *Arts Review*, 42, 14 (13 July 1990), 395–96.

Remy, Michel, 'The Springs of the Firebirds', preface to the catalogue of an exhibition of Emmy Bridgwater's works, London, Blond Fine Art (July 1990).

– 'Devenir et Revenir. Le travail du deuil chez Emmy Bridgwater et Edith Rimmington', in *La Femme s'entête: la part du féminin dans le surréalisme* (Paris: Editions Pleine Marge, Lachenal et Ritter, 1998).

– 'Présentation d'Emmy Bridgwater, surréaliste anglaise', with translations of 12 poems, *Pleine Marge*, 26 (Winter 1997), 25–35.

Ruhl, Mary, 'Uncovering Difference: Emmy Bridgwater and British Surrealism', unpublished dissertation, University of Wolverhampton, School of Humanities and Social Sciences, 1994.

Svensson, Christine, 'The Work of Emmy Bridgwater – An Automatic Thorn in the Flesh of Surrealism', 1994 (unpublished).

Colquhoun, Ithell

'The Double Village', *London Bulletin*, 7 (December 1938–January 1939), 23.

'The Moths', *London Bulletin*, 10 (February 1939), 11.

'What do I need to paint a picture?', 'The Volcano' and 'The Echoing Bruise', *London Bulletin*, 17 (15 June 1939), 13–18.

'Everything Found on Land is Found in the Sea', in *New Road 1943* (Billericay: Grey Walls Press, 1943, 196–99.

'The Mantic Stain', *Enquiry*, 2.4 (October–November 1949), also *Athene* (June 1951).

The Crying of the Wind (London: Peter Owen, 1955).

The Living Stones: Cornwall (London: Peter Owen, 1957).

Goose of Hermogenes (London: Peter Owen, 1961).

Grimoire of the Entangled Thicket (Stevenage: Ore Publications, 1973).

Ramsden, E.H., 'Introduction', catalogue of an exhibition, London, Mayor Gallery (5–29 March 1947).

Young, Andrew McLaren, 'Introduction', catalogue of an exhibition, City of Exeter Museums and Art Gallery (1972).

Davies, Hugh Sykes

Petron (London: Dent, 1935).

'In the Stump of the Old Tree', *Contemporary Poetry and Prose*, 7 (November 1936), 129.

'It Doesn't Look Like...', *London Bulletin*, 2 (May 1938), 7.

'Sympathies with Surrealism', *New Verse*, 8 (April–May 1936), 12–18.

'Surrealism at This Time and Place', in *Surrealism*, ed. Herbert Read (London: Faber and Faber, 1936), 117–68.

'Biology and Surrealism', *International Surrealist Bulletin*, 4 (September 1936), 13–15.

Gascoyne, David, '*Petron*', *New Verse*, 18 (December 1935).

Read, Herbert, '*Petron*', New English Weekly, 8.5 (14 November 1935), 91–92 (with exchange of letters in the 28 November issue).

Del Renzio, Toni

Arson: An Ardent Review, part one of a surrealist manifestation (London, March 1942).

'Surrealist Section', in *New Road 1943* (Billericay: Grey Walls Press, 1943), 180–230.

Incendiary Innocence (London, publ. Toni del Renzio, April 1944).

'The Return to the Desolation', *Arson* (March 1942), 22.

'The Uncouth Invasion: The Paintings of Emmy Bridgwater', *Arson* (March 1942), 24.

'Letter from London', in 'View Listens', *View*, 3, ser. 2 (October 1942), 30.

'Can You Change a Shilling?', *View*, 3, ser. 3 (1943), 83.

'The Light That Will Cease to Fail', in *New Road 1943* (Billericay: Grey Walls Press, 1943), 180–83.

'Surrealism... Or Else', *Tribune* (14 July 1944), 17.

'André Breton a-t-il dit Passe?', *Horizon*, 1, 88 (May 1947), 297–301.

'The Absent Text – The Third Manifesto of Surrealism or Nothing Else', in catalogue of the *Surrealism in England* exhibition (Canterbury: Canterbury College of Art, 1986), 58–64.

'Un Faucon et un Vrai', in *Surrealism – Surrealist Visuality*, ed. Silvano Levy (Keele: Keele University Press, 1995).

'The Exhibitionist, His Overcoat, Several Fetishes and a Phantom or So: The Life and Dreams of Conroy Maddox', in *Conroy Maddox: Surreal Enigmas*, ed. Silvano Levy (Keele: Keele University Press, 1995), 172–77.

Earnshaw, Anthony

Musrum (with Eric Thacker) (London: Jonathan Cape, 1968).

Wintersol (with Eric Thacker) (London: Jonathan Cape, 1971).

Seven Secret Alphabets (London: Jonathan Cape, 1972).

Flick Knives and Forks (Harpford: TRANSFORMAcTION, 1981).

Carping and Kicking (Paris: Hourglass Press, 1987).

Aspects des Bas Quartiers (Paris: Camouflage Press, 1987).

An Eighth Secret Alphabet (Oxford: Hanborough Press, 1987).

Coleman, Les (ed.), *Anthony Earnshaw, The Imp of Surrealism* (Sheffield: RGAP, 2011). Texts by Michel Remy, Gail Earnshaw, Dawn Ades, Michael Richardson, George Hardie, Paul Hammond, Roger Sabin, James Heartfield and Patrick Hughes, Les Coleman and Chris Vine.

Gascoyne, David

Roman Balcony (London: Lincoln Williams, 1932).

Opening Day (London: Cobden-Sanderson, 1932).

A Short Survey of Surrealism (London: Cobden-Sanderson, 1935).

Man's Life is This Meat (London: Parton Press, 1936).

Hölderlin's Madness (London: J.M. Dent, 1938).

Poems 1936–1942 (London: Poetry London Editions, Nicholson and Watson, 1942).

Collected Poems, ed. Robin Skelton (London: Oxford University Press, 1965; new edn, 1988).

Paris Journal 1937–1939, with a preface by Lawrence Durrell (London: Enitharmon Press, 1978).

Paris Journal 1936–1937 (London: Enitharmon Press, 1980).

'Premier Manifeste Anglais du Surréalisme (fragment)', *Cahiers d'Art*, 10 (1935), 106.

'Answers to an Enquiry', *New Verse*, 11 (October 1934), 11–13.

'Petron', *New Verse*, 18 (December 1935).

Benford, Colin T., *David Gascoyne – A Bibliography 1929–1985* (Ryde, Isle of Wight: Heritage Books, 1986).

Cronin, Anthony, 'Poetry and Ideas: David Gascoyne', *London Magazine* (July 1957), 49–55.

Duclos, Michèle, *David Gascoyne*, a special issue of *Cahiers sur la Poésie* (Université de Bordeaux III (GERB), 1986).

Jennings, Elizabeth, 'The Restoration of Symbols', *Twentieth-Century Literature*, 165 (1959), 567–77.

Raine, Kathleen, 'David Gascoyne and the Prophetic Role', *Adam International*, 301 (1966), 41–71. Also *Sewanee Review*, 75.2 (1967), 193–229.

Remy, Michel, *David Gascoyne ou l'urgence de l'inexprimé* (Nancy: Presses Universitaires de Nancy, 1984).

Stanford, Derek, 'David Gascoyne: A Spiritual Itinerary', *Month*, new series, 29.1 (1963), 156–69.

– 'David Gascoyne and the Unacademics', *Meanjin*, 23 (1964), 70–79.
Tolley, A.T., *The Poetry of the Thirties* (London: Gollancz, 1975), 231–40.

Haile, Thomas Samuel

'London's Loss Our Gain', *Art News* (1 March 1944).
'Of Art, the Artist and World War II', *Tomorrow* (November 1944), 129–31 and (December 1944), 153–54.
Clark, Garth, 'Sam Haile 1909–1948: A Memorial', *Studio Potter*, 7.1 (1978), 4–9.
Remy, Michel, 'Samuel Haile's Pursuit of Theory: The Hidden Face of British Surrealism', in catalogue of an exhibition of Haile's works, London, Birch and Conran Gallery (14 October–6 November 1987).
Sewter, A.C., 'T.S. Haile, Potter and Painter', *Apollo* (December 1946), 160–63.

Jennings, Humphrey

'Surrealism', *Contemporary Poetry and Prose*, 8 (December 1936), 167.
'In Magritte's Paintings', *London Bulletin*, 1 (April 1938), 15.
'The Iron Horse', *London Bulletin*, 3 (June 1938), 22, 27–28.
'Do Not Lean Out of the Window', *London Bulletin*, 4–5 (July 1938), 13-1' and 43–44.
'A Determination Not to Dream', *London Bulletin*, 4–5 (July 1938), 40.
'Who Does That Remind You Of?', *London Bulletin*, 6 (October 1938), 21–22.

Films (dating from the surrealist period)

The Birth of the Robot, Shell-Mex and BP Ltd, prod. and dir. Len Lye, sets and prod. H. Jennings (1935–36), 6 min.
Penny Journey, GPO Film Unit, dir. H. Jennings (1938), 8 min.
Design for Spring, dir. H. Jennings (1938), 20 min.
Speaking from America, GPO Film Unit, prod. Alberto Cavalcanti, dir. H. Jennings (1939), 18 min.
Spare Time, GPO Film Unit, prod. Alberto Cavalcanti, dir. H. Jennings (1939).
The First Days, GPO Film Unit, prod. Alberto Cavalcanti, dir. H. Jennings, Harry Watt, Pat Jackson (1939), 20 min.
Belmans, Jacques, *Humphrey Jennings 1907–1950* (Paris: Anthologie du Cinéma, Avant-Scène du Cinéma, 1970).
Bronowski, Julius, *Recollections from Humphrey Jennings* (London: British Film Institute, 1950).
Grierson, John (and Kathleen Raine, Basil Wright, Dilys Powell, Ian Dalrymple, John Greenwood), *Humphrey Jennings, a Tribute* (London: Humphrey Jennings Memorial Fund Committee, n.d.).
Jennings, Mary-Lou (ed.), *Humphrey Jennings, Film-Maker, Painter, Poet* (London: British Film Institute in association with Riverside Studios, 1982).
Lovell, Alan, *Humphrey Jennings* (London: British Film Institute, 1960).
Remy, Michel, 'The Engine Driver in the Forest of Signs: Humphrey Jennings and Surrealism', in *Fifty-third Aldeburgh Festival of Music and the Arts* (9–25 June 2000) (Aldeburgh: Aldeburgh Productions, 2000), 203–207.
– *Humphrey Jennings' 'Imaginative Materialism' or The Mythopoetics of the Machine* (Colchester: Firstsite, 2012).
Von Kassel Siambiani, Elena, *Humphrey Jennings, le poète du cinéma britannique* (Paris: L'Harmattan, 2008).

Lye, Len
No Trouble (Deya, Majorca: Seizin Press, 1939).
Figures of Motion – Selected Writings, eds. Wystan Curnow and Roger Horrocks (Auckland: Auckland University Press/Oxford University Press, 1984).
'Song Time', *London Bulletin*, 18–20 (June 1940), 33.
'Knife Apple Sheer Brush', *The Tiger's Eye* (New York), 7 (March 1948).
'Song Time Stuff', *Life and Letters Today*, 18.11 (Spring 1938) and 18.12 (Summer 1938).
Films
Tusalava, London Film Society (1929), 9 min.
Colour Box, GPO Film Unit (1935), 5 min.
Kaleidoscope, Gerald Noxon and P.W.P. Productions (1935), 4 min.
The Birth of the Robot (with H. Jennings), prod. Shell-Mex and BP Ltd (1935–36), 6 min.
Rainbow Dance, GPO Film Unit (1936), 4 min.
In Time with Industry, GPO Film Unit (1937), 5 min.
Trade Tattoo, GPO Film Unit (1937), 5 min.
North by Northwest (1937), 7 min.
Colour Flight, Imperial Airways (1937), 4 min.
Swinging the Lambeth Walk, Ministry of Information (1939), 4 min.
Len Lye, a Personal Mythology: Paintings, Steel Motion Compositions, Films (Auckland: Auckland City Art Gallery, 1980). Contributions by Andrew Bogle, Gerhard Bauer and Roger Horrocks.

Maddox, Conroy
'The Object in Surrealism', *London Bulletin*, 18–20 (June 1940), 39–45.
'From The Exhibitionist's Overcoat', *Arson* (March 1942), 21.
'From Infiltrations of the Marvellous', *Kingdom Come*, 3.11 (Winter 1942), 16–18.
'From The Exhibitionist's Overcoat', in *New Road 1943* (Billericay: Grey Walls Press, 1943) 212–13.
'Notes on the Christian Myth', *Free Unions Libres* (Summer 1946), 14–15.
Hendry, J.F., 'The Apocalyptic Element in Conroy Maddox', *Kingdom Come*, 3 (Winter 1942), 14–16.
Levy, Silvano (ed.), *Conroy Maddox: Surreal Enigmas* (Keele: Keele University Press, 1995). Texts by Michel Remy, Roger Cardinal, Toni del Renzio, George Melly, Desmond Morris, R.S. Short, Linda Talbot and Simon Wilson.
Remy, Michel, 'Perspectives de la déviance: la peinture surréaliste de Conroy Maddox', *Annales du GERB* (Bordeaux: Université de Bordeaux III), 7 (1989), 107–34.

Mednikoff, Reuben
Catalogue of the exhibition *Grace Pailthorpe and Reuben Mednikoff*, London, Oliver Bradbury and James Birch Fine Art Gallery (13 April–12 May 1984).
Catalogue of the exhibition *Sluice Gates of the Mind: The Collaborative Work of Dr Grace W. Pailthorpe and Reuben Mednikoff*, Leeds, Leeds City Art Gallery (14 January–15 March 1998). Texts by Nigel Walsh, Andrew Wilson, David Maclagan and Michel Remy.

Melly, George
'Mabel's Dream' and 'Poem', *Free Unions Libres* (Summer 1946), 12 and 38.
Rum, Bum and Concertina (London: Weidenfeld and Nicolson, 1977).
Don't Tell Sybil (London: Heinemann, 1997).
'What's Become of Surrealism?', *Vogue*, 122.3 (15 October 1961), 165.

'The Pope of Surrealism', *Observer* (8 March 1970), 8–13.
'The W.C. Fields of Surrealism', *Sunday Times* (15 August 1971), 23–27.

Mesens, E.L.T.

Idolatry and Confusion (with J.B. Brunius) (London: London Gallery Editions, March 1944).

Troisième Front/Third Front, war poems, together with Pièces Détachées, illus. by the author (London: London Gallery Editions, 1944).

Poèmes 1923–1958 (Paris: Le Terrain Vague, 1958).

Geurts-Krauss, Christiane, *E.L.T. Mesens, l'alchimiste méconnu du surréalisme* (Brussels: Editions Labor, 1998).

Jaguer, Edouard, 'Au Pays des Images Défendues', *Aujourd'hui*, 5 (June 1971), 23–27.

Melly, George, 'The W.C. Fields of Surrealism', *Sunday Times* (15 August 1971), 23–27.

Remy, Michel, 'Les années londoniennes de E.L.T. Mesens, ou l'apache dans le vallon', in the catalogue of the exhibition *The Star Alphabet of E.L.T. Mesens*, Ostend, MUZEE (July–November 2013).

TRANSFORMAcTION, ed. John Lyle, special issue in homage to E.L.T. Mesens. Texts by John Lyle, Louis Scutenaire, Roland Penrose, Alberto Cavalcanti, J.M. Matthews, José Pierre, Edouard Jaguer, Enrico Baj and E.L.T. Mesens.

Pailthorpe, Grace W.

Studies in the Psychology of Delinquency (London: Medical Research Council, Special Reports series, 170, 1932).

What We Put in Prison and in Preventive and Rescue Homes (London: Williams and Norgate, 1932).

'The Eye', *transition*, 26 (1937).

'The Scientific Aspects of Surrealism', *London Bulletin*, 7 (December 1938–January 1939), 10–16.

Catalogue of the exhibition *Grace Pailthorpe and Reuben Mednikoff*, London, Oliver Bradbury and James Birch Fine Art Gallery (13 April–12 May 1984).

Catalogue of the exhibition *Sluice Gates of the Mind: The Collaborative Work of Dr Grace W. Pailthorpe and Reuben Mednikoff*, Leeds, Leeds City Art Gallery (14 January–15 March 1998). Texts by Nigel Walsh, Andrew Wilson, David Maclagan and Michel Remy.

Penrose, Roland

'The Transparent Mirror' and 'The Battle of Gloucester', *London Bulletin*, 2 (May 1938), 24 and 4–5 (July 1938), 40.

The Road is Wider than Long (London: London Gallery Editions, 1939).

Home Guard Manual of Camouflage (London: Routledge and Sons, 1941).

In the Service of the People (London: Heinemann, 1945).

Pablo Picasso (London: Gollancz, 1958).

Man Ray (London: Thames and Hudson, 1975).

Scrapbook (London: Thames and Hudson, 1982).

Gascoyne, David, 'A Short Survey of Surrealism', *Axis*, 5 (Spring 1936), 28–30.

– 'Roland Penrose', in the catalogue of the exhibition *Collages Récents*, Paris, Galerie Henriette Gomès (1982).

Lynton, Norbert, introduction to the catalogue of Roland Penrose's retrospective exhibition, London, Institute of Contemporary Arts (London: Arts Council of Great Britain, 1980).

Magritte, René and Nougé, Paul, 'Colour-colours, an Experiment by Roland Penrose', *London Bulletin*, 17 (15 June 1939), 9–10.

Penrose, Antony, *Roland Penrose, the Friendly Surrealist* (Munich, London, New York: Prestel Publishing; Edinburgh: National Galleries of Scotland, 2001).

Rimmington, Edith

Remy, Michel, 'Les Corps abymés d'Edith Rimmington', *Annales du GERB* (Bordeaux: Université de Bordeaux III), 12 (1994).

– 'Devenir et Revenir. Le travail du deuil chez Emmy Bridgwater et Edith Rimmington', in *La Femme s'entête: la part du féminin dans le surréalisme* (Paris: Editions Pleine Marge/Lachenal et Ritter, 1998).

Roughton, Roger

'Surrealism and Communism', *Contemporary Poetry and Prose*, 4 (August–September 1936), 74–75.

'Fascism Murders Art', *Contemporary Poetry and Prose*, 6 (October 1936), 106.

'The Journey', *Contemporary Poetry and Prose*, 8 (December 1936), 152–54.

'The Largest Imaginary Ballroom in the World – A Date at the Kremlin', *Contemporary Poetry and Prose*, 10 (Spring 1937), 33–39.

'The Human House', *Horizon*, 6.19 (July 1941), 50–57.

Watson Taylor, Simon

Free Unions Libres (ed.) (summer 1946).

'Fragments from My Real Life in Exact Proportion to Those Who Cannot Read…', *Free Unions Libres* (summer 1946), 18–19.

Welson, John W.

Water Throat: The Paintings, Drawings and Poems of John Welson, with an introduction by Robert Golden (London, privately printed, 1982).

'The Surrealist Proposition', in *Surrealism, the Hinge of History* (Melmoth; London: Freedom Press, 1978).

Maddox, Conroy, 'For John Welson', in the catalogue of the exhibition *John Welson: Drawings and Paintings*, London, Crashaw Gallery (25–29 April 1990).

Remy, Michel, 'John Welson', in the catalogue of the exhibition *John Welson: Drawings and Paintings*, London, Crashaw Gallery (25–29 April 1990).

General Index

237

Index of Poem Titles and First Lines

Titles are in italics, first lines in roman type